GLORIOUSTINA ESSIA

AI Secrets for the Creator Economy

200+ Proven ways to make money from AI in 2024

Contents

I

AI Secrets for the Creator Economy 200+ Proven ways to make money from AI in 2024

Introduction

Welcome to a new world where limitless creativity collides with the limitless potential of Artificial Intelligence (AI) to transform the core of the Creator Economy. The Creator Economy, an ever-changing digital world, is reaching new heights. It is a field where the convergence of artistic ability, entrepreneurial ambition, and the revolutionary power of AI has resulted in a deep synergy of possibility. This fusion of human talent and machine intelligence has created a world where creators can use AI's untapped potential to achieve wealth and personal joy.

"AI Secrets for the Creator Economy: 200+ Proven Ways to Make Money from AI in 2024" is a compass to guide you through this AI-powered landscape, where innovation, financial prosperity, and personal growth intersect in unprecedented ways.

Activating the Creator Economy

The Creator Economy, a rapidly growing digital phenomenon, has reached a tipping point. Many talents—YouTubers, podcasters, artists, musicians, educators, and influencers—have established their distinct niches within its world. They create their identities, grow their businesses, and turn their hobbies into profitable ventures here. Entrepreneurship has defied tradition in this day and age, allowing innovators to direct their destinies.

2024 marks a watershed moment in which AI will become indispensable within this ecosystem. AI is not a passive tool; instead, it is a catalyst for invention, a magnifier of efficiency, and a speedy monetization accelerator. AI is not a bystander; it works with artists to make their most extraordinary visions a reality.

Unlocking the AI Secrets

At the centre of this transforming trip is a goldmine of "AI Secrets for the Creator Economy." This book goes beyond mere knowledge acquisition; it serves as a road map for navigating the complicated terrain of AI. It covers everything from fundamental AI principles to advanced applications, making it accessible to people with various technical backgrounds. This resource keeps you at the forefront of AI expertise in a setting where AI is constantly evolving.

A plethora of Opportunities

"AI Secrets for the Creator Economy" is your guide to solving AI's enigma. It demonstrates the several ways in which AI can help you create more money in the Creator Economy, shedding light on the following domains:

Content Creation and Enhancement: Explore AI-powered content generation, where text, images, videos, and music are no longer simply the domain of human producers. AI transforms into a dependable collaborator, transforming your work and releasing untapped creative potential.

Audience Involvement and Growth: The fundamental element of success is genuine involvement with your audience. AI becomes your strategic collaborator, providing insights into audience preferences and cultivating genuine connections that result in unrivalled influence and engagement.

Monetization tactics: Monetization is more than just profit; it is about optimizing tactics with AI. Discover how artificial intelligence improves income generation, whether through subscription models, advertising, or e-commerce, converting viewers into devoted customers.

Entrepreneurship & Business Development: Investigate funding options, learn from success stories, and avoid common traps to pave the road for a successful entrepreneurial journey.

Making Your Creator Economy Future-Proof Career: Success is not a destination; it is an ongoing journey. As we look to the future, we predict AI trends for 2024 and beyond. This trip is about more than just making money; it emphasizes the importance of using AI responsibly and navigating ethical landscapes.

As you read "AI Secrets for the Creator Economy: 200+ Proven Ways to Make Money from AI in 2024," you start on a transforming adventure. The AI secrets you discover within these pages will unleash a world in which innovation, creativity, and financial success coexist to exceed your most ambitious goals. It's time to release the AI secrets and begin on a path of transformational success.

The Creator Economy

1.1 The Creator Economy: A New Era in Digital Entrepreneurship

The digital world of the twenty-first century has seen a seismic upheaval in how people develop, share, and sell their talents, skills, and hobbies. The Creator Economy, a dynamic and ever-evolving ecosystem that has democratized entrepreneurship, allowing individuals to reclaim control of their lives and harness the power of the internet to develop lucrative and rewarding jobs, is at the heart of this change. Understanding the Creator Economy's significant impact on our society and the global economy requires defining it.

The Unveiling of the Creator Economy

The Creator Economy, also known as the Passion Economy or the Passion-preneur Movement, symbolizes a paradigm shift in how people earn money and build a career as digital entrepreneurs. It is a world in which people with varied talents, interests, and creative abilities use digital platforms and technology to reach a worldwide audience. This audience can range from a few devoted followers to millions of ardent supporters.

The collapse of traditional gatekeepers is one of the Creator Economy's defining traits. Obtaining access to large audiences and monetizing artistic pursuits used to necessitate approval from established institutions or businesses. Anyone with a desire and the means to create content may become an independent creator and develop a successful career without the need for intermediaries. This paradigm change enables creators to become their bosses, personal brand CEOs, and custodians of their creative journeys.

Digital Age Innovators

Creators in the digital age include a diverse range of people and professions. YouTubers, podcasters, bloggers, writers, artists, musicians, educators, and influencers are among them. They can create a wide range of content using digital resources, from films and essays to music and art. Creators from all walks of life are welcome in the Creator Economy, regardless of background, age, or location. This openness is a motivating reason behind the movement's rapid expansion.

Making Money from Your Creativity

The monetization of creative labour is a critical component of the Creator Economy. Advertisements, sponsored content, item sales, subscription models, and direct support from their audience are all ways for creators to make money. These revenue streams provide financial security and allow creators to convert their passion into a vocation.

Creating and Engaging Communities

In the Creator Economy, engagement and community-building are critical to success. Through interactions, discussions, and social media platforms, creators cultivate relationships with their audience. This strong bond creates devoted fans who not only watch material but also actively support authors through likes, shares, comments, and monetary contributions.

Content is Currency

The money in the Creator Economy is content. Creators put in time and effort to create material that resonates with their audience, and this content is critical to establishing their brand and earning money. The material is suited to the tastes of the creator's niche, whether informational, entertaining, inspirational, or instructional.

The Impact of AI and Technology

Technology, particularly Artificial Intelligence (AI), plays a vital role in the evolution of the Creator Economy. Artificial intelligence-powered tools and platforms help creators in various ways, from content development and optimization to audience analysis and revenue. AI has evolved into an essential collaborator for creators, providing solutions to streamline procedures and improve the quality and efficiency of their work.

In a nutshell, the Creator Economy is a digital revolution that allows individuals to commercialize their creativity and passions without the need for traditional institutions or intermediaries. It represents a new era of business and financial independence in which creators are central to their success stories. As the Creator Economy evolves, integrating technology, AI, and digital platforms will play an essential role in moulding its future, providing creators with new opportunities and methods for success.

1.2 The Interplay of AI and Creativity

The interaction between Artificial Intelligence (AI) and creativity has emerged as a dynamic force in the fast-expanding digital landscape, transforming how we create, innovate, and express ourselves. This synergy, also known as human-machine collaboration, has ushered in a new era in which AI's computational prowess augments human inventiveness. This marriage of artificial intelligence and creativity is reshaping businesses, enabling artists and entrepreneurs, and transforming how we perceive and interact with the world.

AI's Creative Ability

Once restricted to data analysis and automation, artificial intelligence has exceeded its early constraints. AI now exhibits a surprising ability for creative jobs. Machine learning algorithms, deep learning networks, and natural language processing models have been used to create art, music, literature, and design frequently indistinguishable from human-created creations.

AI-powered generative adversarial networks (GANs) create paintings, illustrations, and animations that fascinate and intrigue the field of visual arts. AI may make music that crosses genres, imitate classical composers, or generate new soundscapes. Even in storytelling, AI may generate prose that mimics the styles of famous authors or create wholly unique storylines. These creative initiatives result from AI's ability to analyze large datasets, learn patterns, and produce material with a human touch.

AI as the Collaborative Muse

The ability of AI to serve as a collaborative muse makes AI's engagement in creativity so fascinating. Instead of replacing human artists, AI is a collaborator, a source of inspiration, and a tool for pushing the limits of human imagination. The interaction of human creativity and AI has resulted in ground-breaking advancements in various creative fields.

Consider the field of music composition, where AI systems aid musicians in the creation of complicated compositions and the exploration of new sounds. Musicians can venture into unexplored musical territory by incorporating AI-generated melodies, harmonies, and rhythms into their works, infusing them with a unique blend of human and machine brilliance.

In the visual arts, AI augments artists' abilities by assisting them in refining and visualizing their ideas. Image modification is aided by AI technologies, which allow artists to experiment with numerous styles, effects, and upgrades. Artists can use AI to bring digital canvases to life, blurring the line between traditional and digital art.

AI as an Innovation Catalyst

The interaction between AI and creativity is not restricted to traditional artistic pursuits. It encompasses many businesses, from healthcare and finance to education and entertainment. Artificial intelligence-powered solutions are transforming data analysis, automating repetitive operations, and improving decision-making processes. AI-powered analytics in business provide insights into customer behaviour and market trends, enabling entrepreneurs to make informed decisions and develop new strategies.

AI is used in healthcare to evaluate medical imaging, uncover patterns in patient data, and aid in diagnosis. Combining artificial intelligence's analytical skills with human medical experience results in more accurate diagnoses and novel treatment options.

AI-Assisted Content Creation

Content creators, a significant force in the Creator Economy, profit from AI's creative potential as well. Artificial intelligence-powered solutions accelerate content production and optimization, allowing producers to produce high-quality material more effectively. AI helps in the creative process, whether writing articles, editing films, or designing visuals.

1.3 Why AI is the Locomotive for Success: A Revolution in Progress

The path to success has undergone a radical shift in the twenty-first century, with Artificial Intelligence (AI) emerging as the essential engine propelling individuals, corporations, and sectors to unprecedented heights of achievement. AI is more than just a tool; it is a disruptive force redefining how we work, innovate, and function. It has a profound and far-reaching impact on various industries, from technology to healthcare, creative arts to finance. Let's examine why artificial intelligence has become the driving force behind success in the digital age.

Increased Productivity and Efficiency

One of the most apparent reasons why AI is a successful locomotive is its capacity to improve efficiency and production drastically. Automation and task optimization powered by AI reduce the time and effort necessary for ordinary and challenging jobs. AI systems can handle data analysis, content development, and customer support with outstanding speed and accuracy, allowing human workers to focus on higher-value jobs. This results in a significant boost in productivity, which is a crucial driver of success in any industry.

Exceptional Data Analysis and Insights

The ability of AI to analyze data is a significant change in today's corporate world. AI systems can process massive amounts of data in real time, revealing patterns, trends, and valuable insights that humans may miss. AI enables decision-makers in industries such as marketing, finance, and healthcare to make data-driven decisions, improving the precision and effectiveness of their plans.

Customer Experience and Personalization

The driving force behind the individualized experiences that customers and users have come to anticipate is artificial intelligence. It powers recommendation engines, chatbots, and virtual assistants that personalize encounters. In e-commerce, for example, AI-powered product recommendations boost sales by giving customers precisely what they desire. Personalization fosters engaged audiences and dedicated followers in content creation, laying the groundwork for success in the Creator Economy.

Creative Augmentation and Innovation

AI is more than simply automation and analysis; it is also a source of invention and creative enhancement. AI tools support and motivate artists to explore new horizons in creative professions such as painting, music, and design. AI can help entrepreneurs and inventors discover new ideas and streamline operations. AI is no longer replacing human creativity; rather, it is supplementing it, improving human potential, and enabling inventive discoveries.

Capabilities for Prediction

The capacity to forecast future patterns and consequences is critical to success. Whether it's anticipating market trends, predicting disease outbreaks, or improving supply networks, AI is a prediction master. With AI, organizations and people can make more confident strategic decisions and capture opportunities.

Ease of Access and Inclusion

AI is becoming more accessible, allowing more people to harness its power. This inclusiveness is fueling success in domains like education, where AI-powered tools aid in tailored learning, and entrepreneurship, where AI-powered platforms democratize access to resources and possibilities.

Adaptation and Lifelong Learning

In an ever-changing world, the capacity to adapt and learn on the fly is vital to success. AI systems are built to learn from new data, adapt to changing conditions, and stay current on the newest trends and technology. Individuals and organizations with this adaptability can stay at the forefront of their industries, assuring long-term success.

Monetization and Wealth Creation

AI is an excellent asset-generation technique, particularly in the Creator Economy. AI can help content creators, entrepreneurs, and enterprises optimize their monetization strategies, whether they use subscription models, advertising, or e-commerce. AI improves user experiences and customer engagement, resulting in financial success.

The significance of AI as a successful locomotive cannot be emphasized. Its potential to increase efficiency, provide deep insights, personalize, drive innovation, forecast outcomes, create inclusivity, and enable adaptability is altering industries and human lives. In an era where data-driven decision-making, personalization, and innovation are critical, artificial intelligence (AI) has emerged as the driving force propelling individuals and enterprises to new heights of performance. In a world where the possibilities are endless, success in the digital age is becoming synonymous with the efficient use of AI.

II

Content Creation and Enhancement

AI-Powered Content Generation

2.1 The Art and Science of AI-Generated Content: Bridging the Gap Between Creativity and Technology

The interaction of art and science in the age of the Creator Economy and the digital revolution has given rise to a phenomenon that challenges conventional concepts of creativity—the development of content by Artificial Intelligence (AI). This marriage of art and science unleashes a transformational power, opening new avenues for content creation, innovation, and communication. To comprehend the art and science of AI-generated material, one must investigate the junction between human creativity and AI's computational capabilities.

AI as the Digital Muse

AI-generated material, whether text, photographs, music, or videos, demonstrates the power of machine learning and deep learning models. These AI systems are more than just tools; they have evolved into muses, inspiring new levels of creativity. The ability of AI to understand patterns, mimic styles, and generate content that is nearly indistinguishable from human-created works distinguishes it from traditional software.

Opening Up New Artistic Frontiers

AI has become a creative partner, pushing the bounds of human imagination. AI tools in the visual arts assist artists by generating designs, modifying photos, and even inventing new visual concepts. Musicians explore with artificial intelligence-generated melodies, harmonies, and rhythms, resulting in songs that challenge traditional genres and approaches. AI writes prose and poetry in the literary realm, sometimes collaborating with human authors to co-create unique storylines.

The Role of AI in Content Creation

The art and science of AI-generated content include a broad range of content types:

AI-generated articles, blog entries, and reports are becoming more common. The topics covered by these AI-written writings span from news and sports to scientific research and creative narrative.

AI-powered picture production and manipulation are standard in design, photography, and digital art. AI is also a crucial participant in the creation of video content, creating animations, special effects, and even deep fake films.

Music and Audio Content: AI plays a significant part in the music industry, from composition and arrangement to sound engineering. It generates one-of-a-kind soundscapes, tailored music playlists, and even AI-powered music compositions.

Increasing Productivity and Efficiency

AI-generated content is a game changer in efficiency and production, not just creative creativity. AI solutions are used by content creators, marketers, and organizations to automate content creation, streamline production processes, and provide highly tailored content to target audiences. This saves time while also ensuring consistency and relevancy.

AI as a Creative Collaborator

Ultimately, AI-generated content serves as a reminder that machines will not replace human creators in the future of creativity. Instead, AI is a collaborator and a tool to augment human brilliance. It boosts creativity, opens up new frontiers and possibilities, and changes how we think about content creation. The art and science of AI-generated content demonstrate that combining human creativity with AI's computational skills can result in an inspirational and transformative union in which the borders between artist and machine blur and the future of content production is infinite.

2.2 AI in Written Content Production: The Future Digital Scribe

The role of Artificial Intelligence (AI) in the fast-expanding environment of content creation has grown increasingly important, transforming the way written content is generated, edited, and delivered.

Content Creation Tools Powered by AI

Artificial intelligence-powered content creation tools quickly become indispensable companions for authors, marketers, and enterprises looking to streamline content production. Natural language processing (NLP) and machine learning algorithms are used in these tools to generate written material ranging from news reports and product descriptions to blog articles and social media updates.

The benefits are apparent:

Efficiency: AI can generate vast amounts of content in a fraction of the time that a human writer would. This efficiency is essential for content marketing efforts and breaking news.

AI maintains consistency in tone and style, which is critical for maintaining a coherent brand voice in marketing materials or adhering to editorial requirements in news sites.

Personalization: Artificial intelligence may provide highly personalized content, personalizing messages to individual users based on their tastes, activities, and demographic data.

Multilingual Capabilities: Artificial intelligence content generation tools are not limited by language limitations. They may create material in several languages, increasing the accessibility of global marketing initiatives.

Applications in Journalism and News Reporting

AI is becoming a valuable helper to human reporters in journalism and news reporting. Algorithms for automated news writing can analyze data, generate real-time reporting on stock market swings, weather updates, or sports scores, and even build stories from structured data such as financial reports. This type of AI content synthesis is beneficial when rapid information distribution is required.

SEO Optimization and Content Marketing

AI has added a new layer to content strategy for content marketers. Artificial intelligence (AI) systems can monitor user behaviour, search patterns, and market competition to recommend content ideas that are likely to perform well. This knowledge enables marketers to generate content that is more appealing to their target audience and ranks higher in search engine results.

AI can also optimize material for search engines. It can recommend key-words, analyze text readability, and ensure that material adheres to SEO best practices, increasing its chances of appearing high in search results.

Storytelling and creative writing

The significance of AI goes beyond news and marketing. In creative writing and storytelling, AI is entering territory formerly considered unique to human authors. Artificial intelligence algorithms may generate fictitious stories, poetry, and creative prose, replicating numerous writing styles and genres. Authors and screenwriters increasingly collaborate with artificial intelligence to generate ideas and overcome writer's block.

The Importance of AI in the Production of Written Content

Continuous breakthroughs in NLP, machine learning, and AI-driven content generation tools will shape the future of AI in written content production. AI's role is poised to grow, providing content creators with new prospects for innovation and efficiency. While AI can help with content creation, the human touch is still required for creativity, editorial judgment, and ethical issues. The combination of human intellect and artificial intelligence's computational capability is revolutionizing textual content production, opening up new horizons of possibilities and challenging our understanding of the creative process. In a world where artificial intelligence (AI) is the digital scribe of the future, the lines between humans and machines in content creation continue to blur, creating a landscape where the possibilities are as endless as the digital frontier itself.

2.3 AI in Visual and Multimedia Content Creation: Unleashing the Creative Potential

The integration of artificial intelligence (AI) and creative arts in the digital era has given rise to a transformational force that is transforming the landscape of visual and multimedia content creation. AI is no longer limited to data analysis and automation; it has become a must-have tool for artists, designers, filmmakers, and content creators. The impact of AI in this domain is substantial and far-reaching, opening up many new opportunities and advances.

AI as a Creative Partner

The role of AI in developing visual and multimedia material is one of collaboration rather than replacement. AI systems act as creative collaborators, pushing the limits of human imagination. Instead of replacing human artists, AI aids them in realizing their creative ideas. This confluence between human creativity and AI computational prowess has resulted in game-changing advancements in various creative sectors.

Image Creation and Manipulation

AI-generated material has made inroads into the visual arts. AI-powered technologies can create captivating photos, graphics, and animations. AI can help artists and designers refine and visualize their ideas. Image modification is aided by AI technologies, which allow artists to experiment with numerous styles, effects, and upgrades. As a result, human creativity is combined with AI's precision and computational strength.

AI-Enhanced Video Production

AI's influence on multimedia content generation extends to video production. Artificial intelligence-powered solutions have become essential in video editing, special effects, and post-production workflows. These tools make formerly time-consuming processes easier, allowing filmmakers to focus on the artistic parts of their work. AI also plays a role in video analytics, assisting with video categorization, labelling, and recommendation.

Sound Engineering and Music Composition

AI is changing composition, sound engineering, and music creation in music and audio material. Algorithms powered by AI can generate music in various forms, emulating classical composers or creating new soundscapes. AI-generated melodies, harmonies, and rhythms can be used as inspiration by musicians and producers to create unique and genre-defying music.

Content Recommendation and Personalization

The impact of AI is not confined to content generation; it also extends to content delivery. Personalization, powered by AI, is now an essential component of how users interact with multimedia material. To provide individualized content suggestions, recommendation engines assess user preferences and behaviour. AI plays a critical role in curating material tailored to individual tastes, whether it's on streaming platforms, news websites, or e-commerce storefronts.

AI's Role in Visual and Multimedia Content Creation

The future of AI in visual and multimedia content creation promises to be exciting. AI systems will supplement the creative process as they grow more complex and accessible, providing new tools for artists, designers, and content creators to explore. This transition does not replace human ingenuity but rather extends creative possibilities.

The impact of AI on creating visual and multimedia material demonstrates the potential of human creativity and technical advancement. It changes our thoughts about art, design, cinema, and music production. The boundaries between human and machine in the creative process will continue to blur as AI evolves and collaborates with human creators, ushering in a future where artistic expression knows no bounds and the fusion of human ingenuity and AI computational potential unleashes a new era of creativity and innovation.

2.4 AI and Music Composition in Harmony: A Symphony of Creativity and Technology

Music has always been a powerful reflection of human ingenuity, as a universal language that spans nations and generations. Composers and musicians have created masterpieces that evoke emotions, tell stories, and inspire future generations for millennia. This ancient art form is changing the digital age, with the harmonious combination of Artificial Intelligence (AI) and music composition pushing the frontiers of creativity and innovation.

AI as a Composer's Assistant

In music creation, AI has emerged as a helpful partner, working with human composers to stimulate new creative frontiers. It provides composers a powerful tool for experimenting with, creating, and fine-tuning musical compositions. Instead of replacing composers, AI augments human creativity by generating new ideas, suggesting novel structures, and allowing for the exploration of various styles.

Melodies and Harmonies Created by AI

AI's ability to generate melodies, harmonies, and musical frameworks is one of its most significant contributions to music composition. AI systems learn from classical compositions to modern songs by analyzing enormous musical collections. With this knowledge, AI may compose creative works in various genres, mimicking famous composers or establishing new styles.

Genre and Style Possibilities are Endless

AI in music composition provides endless options. Composers and musicians can experiment with AI-generated compositions in various genres, including classical, jazz, electronic, and experimental music. AI is equally competent at crafting conventional music as it explores avant-garde styles, fostering innovation in the music world.

Improving the Creativity Process

AI helps composers overcome creative blockages by streamlining the music composing process. It may generate musical phrases, chord progressions, and instrumental arrangements, which can be used to start composing. These AI-generated parts can then be shaped and personalized by composers to create their compositions.

Composition of Film Scores and Soundtracks

Artificial intelligence has discovered uses in soundtrack and cinema score composition. Composers and filmmakers work with AI to create music that compliments a film's mood and plot. Artificial intelligence can evaluate the emotional context of scenes and make music that enriches the visual experience. This partnership results in memorable soundtracks that are well-received by audiences.

Sound Design and Music Production

AI is also used in music production and sound design. It aids in noise reduction, audio improvement, and mixing chores in sound engineering. AI-powered tools enable musicians and producers to modify and refine audio aspects novelly.

AI's Role in Music Composition

The future of AI in music creation looks exciting and transformational. AI systems will continue to inspire composers and musicians to push creative boundaries as they grow more sophisticated and accessible. Composers will have many AI tools to explore new sound areas, develop previously unseen harmonies, and write musical stories that engage with audiences.

The harmony of AI and music composition provides an enthralling synthesis of human creativity and technical innovation. In the creative process, AI is a collaborator rather than a substitute, providing composers with new paths for inquiry and experimentation. This collaboration between the artistic soul and the computational mind reshapes the boundaries of music composition, ushering in a future where musical expression knows no bounds. The fusion of human ingenuity and AI's computational potential yields a symphony of creativity and innovation that resonates with the world.

Content Personalization and Optimization

3.1 The Potent Spell of Personalization: Redefining User Experiences

P ersonalization has evolved as a powerful spell that captivates and enchants consumers across numerous platforms in an era marked by the digital revolution and an overwhelming availability of content. Personalization crafts a fascinating web of bespoke experiences that feel made especially for you, whether browsing through your favourite social media feed, shopping online or listening to music. This magic, wielded by the wand of Artificial Intelligence (AI) and machine learning, is reshaping how we interact with digital material and services.

The Age of Customized Experiences

Personalization is more than just customization; it is the art of designing experiences that connect with people on a highly personal level. It learns about users' tastes, behaviours, and previous interactions to present content, product recommendations, and services that feel tailored to them. This level of customization has become a digital age signature, contrasting the information overload and generic content that permeates the online world.

AI as the Enchanter Behind the Curtain

AI, namely machine learning algorithms, is the key to breaking the trap of personalization. These algorithms examine massive amounts of data, ranging from your online behaviour to your demographic information, and utilize this knowledge to anticipate your preferences. AI learns from your interactions, honing its grasp of your preferences and tailoring recommendations accordingly. The more you interact with the system, the more precise and appealing the customization gets.

Social Media and Content Platform Personalization

Personalization is visible in the content displayed on your social media feed. The algorithms ensure that postings from friends, relatives, and pages you engage with receive a prominent placement. Likewise, entertainment platforms like YouTube, Netflix, and Spotify employ personalization to offer videos, movies, and music based on your viewing and listening habits. The outcome is an endlessly fascinating and relevant stream of content.

E-commerce and Product Recommendations

Online buying has been altered by personalization. E-commerce companies employ AI to recommend things based on browsing history, purchasing habits, and even the products you've loved or rated. This not only simplifies the purchasing process but also exposes you to goods you might not have discovered on your own.

Tailored News and Content Curation

News providers and content aggregators embrace personalization to give tailored news and articles. Your interests, location, and past reading behaviour influence the material you view. This guarantees that you receive news relevant to your tastes, which can be particularly beneficial in an age of information saturation.

Personalization's Future

The future of customization promises even more enthralling experiences. AI systems will improve their knowledge of human intent and context, generating material that feels both customized and anticipatory. With the integration of AI in different facets of daily life, the lines between online and offline customization will blur.

The powerful magic of personalization, wielded by AI and machine learning, has reshaped how we interact with digital information and services. It provides consumers with a customized, relevant, and engaging experience that allows them to feel seen, heard, and valued. However, as this spell continues to enchant us, it also requires vigilance in ensuring that the ethical dimensions of personalization are respected and that the magic of customization remains accessible to all, transcending boundaries and delivering delightful digital experiences to users worldwide.

3.2 AI-Driven Content Recommendations: The Future of Personalized Engagement

The function of content suggestions enabled by Artificial Intelligence (AI) has become crucial to our online experiences in today's digital ecosystem, where the influx of content is nearly limitless. These AI-powered content recommendation systems are more than simply valuable ideas; they are the driving forces behind personalized engagement that keeps consumers returning for more. This phenomenon marks a paradigm shift in the way people consume content, making it more relevant and engaging than ever before.

The Power of Personalization

AI-powered content recommendations are the digital equivalent of personalization. These systems assess user behaviour, preferences, and historical interactions using powerful machine learning algorithms. They serve up content that is not only relevant but also interesting to each user by recognizing individual tastes. AI tailors your experience to your interests, whether watching videos, reading news, or purchasing online.

The Principles of AI-Driven Recommendations

The secret sauce of AI-powered content suggestions is data analysis and predictive algorithms. This is how it works:

Data Collection: These systems capture massive amounts of data, such as user clicks, views, likes, dislikes, purchase history, and even mouse movements.

This data serves as the foundation for understanding user behaviour.

Data Analysis: Machine learning algorithms comb the data, looking for patterns and correlations. The computers learn about individual preferences by recognizing the types of information people tend to engage with.

Predictive Recommendations: Once recognized, these patterns are used by AI algorithms to create predictions. They predict what material a user would love next. These are the content recommendations that are shown to the user.

Applications on Multiple Digital Platforms

AI-powered content recommendations can be found on a variety of digital platforms, including:

1. **Streaming Services**: Platforms such as Netflix, Spotify, and YouTube utilize artificial intelligence (AI) to recommend movies, music, and videos based on your viewing and listening history. This customization keeps consumers interested and pushes them to explore new information.

2. **E-commerce:** AI-powered product recommendations are revolutionizing online purchasing. E-commerce websites, such as Amazon, show consumers things they might be interested in, often leading to higher sales and customer happiness.

3. **News Aggregators**: News providers and content aggregators cater to individual preferences. Your reading habits and preferences are used to choose the articles and news stories you see.

4. **Social Media**: Social media systems prioritize material from your most engaged friends, pages, and groups. This guarantees that your feed contains

content that is relevant to your interests.

5. **Online Advertising**: AI suggestions include online advertising. Advertisers use artificial intelligence (AI) to target their adverts to consumers most likely interested in their products or services, enhancing ad efficiency.

The future of AI-powered content suggestions is exciting. Content personalization will become more accurate and anticipatory as AI algorithms get more polished and complicated. AI will not only cater to your current interests but will also predict what you would like to discover in the future. This means content will be customized and coincidental, arousing curiosity and delight.

III

Audience Engagement and Growth

Building Your AI-Powered Audience

4.1 AI for Audience Insights: Illuminating the Path to Effective Communication

U nderstanding your audience is critical to efficient communication in the digital age, where information is abundant and attention spans are short. Audience insights are a compass for content creators, marketers, and businesses to generate messages that appeal to their target groups. In this drive for comprehension, Artificial Intelligence (AI) emerges as a potent instrument capable of decoding audience insights in previously imagined ways.

The Search for Audience Insight

Audience insights include various information, such as demographic data and behavioural tendencies, user preferences and engagement metrics. These observations shed light on who your target audience is, what they want when they want it, and how they want to consume it. They serve as the foundation for individualized and efficient communication.

AI as an Insights Oracle

AI-driven tools and algorithms reveal these insights. They comb through digital traces to identify patterns and trends in massive volumes of data. Here's how the procedure works:

Data collecting: The journey begins with data collecting, which includes user interactions, social media activity, browsing habits, and other factors. This data is the raw material used to create insights.

Data Analysis: Algorithms for machine learning and data analytics deconstruct this data. They can identify behavioural patterns, preferences, and trends. AI lays the groundwork for personalization by recognizing what connects with different audience segments.

Predictive Insights: The true magic occurs when AI leverages these patterns to forecast future behaviour. These forecasts influence content recommendations, ad targeting, and marketing tactics.

AI Applications for Recognizing Audience Insights

AI-powered audience insights have numerous applications in the digital landscape:

Content Personalization: AI insights are used by streaming services, e-commerce platforms, and news aggregators to recommend personalized content. This guarantees that what you see, read, or hear matches your preferences.

AI insights power targeted advertising in marketing and advertising. They allow firms to target the correct audience with the right message, enhancing ad efficiency and ROI.

Product Development: Companies employ audience data to create products that correspond to consumer tastes. AI shows not only what customers say they want but also what their actions disclose about their genuine preferences.

Engagement on Social Media: Social media sites use insights to highlight content in your feed. Posts from friends, pages, and groups you interact with the most are prioritized.

AI-driven audience insights serve as a guidepost for effective communication in the digital age. They assist content creators and businesses in better understanding their audiences, creating tailored experiences, and tailoring their messaging for maximum impact. As AI advances, the depth and accuracy of insights will expand, opening up new avenues for effective communication and ensuring that messages resonate with audiences in meaningful and relevant ways. Pursuing audience insights using AI will continue, exposing the route to effective communication.

4.2 Chatbots and Virtual Assistants Captivating Audiences: The Future of Engagement

The pursuit of audience engagement is a critical task in today's digital landscape. Businesses and content providers resort to novel ways to capture and maintain their audience as information overload competes for fading attention spans. Chatbots and virtual assistants driven by AI emerge as intriguing allies, promising not just to ease work but also to captivate and fascinate audiences with their capacity to give immediate, personalized, and engaging experiences.

Chatbots and Virtual Assistants are on the rise.

Customer service and engagement are evolving, thanks to chatbots and virtual assistants. These AI-powered entities are not only efficient and available 24 hours a day, but they are also exceptionally good at interpreting and reacting to consumer requests. They have progressed from being only information suppliers to becoming personalized companions, enablers, and even entertainment.

Conversational AI's Mysteries

Chatbots and virtual assistants use conversational AI, a technique that allows them to understand, process, and synthesize human-like language. Natural language processing (NLP) decodes user inputs, allowing seamless, human-like interactions. These AI entities' algorithms enable them to recognize user intents and execute tasks with surprising accuracy.

Applications in a Variety of Industries

Chatbots and virtual assistants are enticing people in a variety of industries:

Chatbots and virtual assistants provide instant support and solutions to consumer concerns in customer service. They are available 24 hours a day, seven days a week, removing the need to wait for human assistance.

E-commerce: These AI entities have transformed online purchasing. They aid users with product selection, recommendations, and even purchases, increasing the whole shopping experience.

Chatbots and virtual assistants are being used in healthcare for symptom assessment, prescription reminders, and even emotional support. They increase patient engagement and help to improve health outcomes.

Chatbots and virtual assistants in the entertainment industry can provide personalized content recommendations, assist with ticket purchases, and engage users in fun banter, generating memorable encounters.

Content Discovery: These AI entities are skilled at finding relevant content. They recommend articles, videos, and music based on user preferences and previous interactions in media and content platforms.

Personalization and engagement have been improved.

The capacity of chatbots and virtual assistants to personalize user experiences is one of their key capabilities. They learn from encounters and use this knowledge to offer tailored recommendations, provide relevant information, and engage in conversations tailored to the individual.

Audience Engagement with AI Entities in the Future

Chatbots and virtual assistants have a bright future in attracting and mesmerizing audiences. As AI advances, these beings' interactions will become ever more intuitive, predictive, and human-like. They will blend into our daily lives and become necessary partners.

Chatbots and virtual assistants powered by AI are transforming how businesses and content providers interact with their audiences. Their capacity to deliver quick, tailored, and engaging encounters distinguishes them as enablers of fascinating, seamless engagements. As AI technology advances, these AI entities are poised to captivate audiences in ways that redefine the concept of engagement, transforming them from tools to vital companions capable of offering captivating and fulfilling experiences.

4.3 AI as a Vibrant Community Architect: Creating a Better Digital Society

Artificial Intelligence (AI) has emerged as a formidable force in the age of rapid technological growth, with the ability to impact the future of our digital society. AI is increasingly important in developing lively and networked communities, in addition to its uses in automation and data processing. It designs digital neighbourhoods, creating locations for individuals to interact, share, and prosper.

The Digital Communities of Today

Digital communities have become an essential part of our daily lives. They include social media networks, online forums, collaborative workspaces, and similar services. These areas function as communication, knowledge-sharing, and cooperation hubs. They do, however, require a level of organization, administration, and personalization that might take more work to achieve at scale to remain active and vital.

Artificial Intelligence as a Connector

AI serves as the digital bridge that unites individuals inside these digital communities. Here's how it's done:

Personalization occurs when AI systems examine user data to determine preferences, habits, and needs. They utilize this information to tailor the user experience. For example, social media companies utilize AI to prioritize information in users' feeds, ensuring that posts from their most engaged friends, groups, or pages are prominently highlighted.

AI can help with content curation and suggestions. It assists users in discovering relevant material, such as news articles, videos, or items. AI refines its recommendations by evaluating user interactions and feedback, ensuring that users are exposed to information relevant to their interests.

AI can monitor internet communities, recognizing and correcting concerns such as spam, harassment, or improper content. It provides a safe and welcoming environment for users by automating these operations.

Chatbots and virtual assistants help to increase community engagement. They respond to user inquiries, supply information, and even engage in light chat, providing a sense of community even in virtual places.

Applications on Multiple Digital Platforms

AI has an impact on a wide range of digital platforms:

Social media networks, such as Facebook and Twitter, use AI to personalize content, filter spam, and detect fraudulent accounts and misinformation. This ensures that consumers interact with authentic material and connect with others who share their interests.

Online forums and discussion boards employ AI to moderate content, ensuring that debates are civil and respectful. Artificial intelligence systems recognize and filter out hazardous comments.

Collaborative Workspaces: Platforms like Slack and Microsoft Teams use artificial intelligence to boost productivity. Intelligent search, automatic file organization, and even project management aids are available, making collaboration more accessible and efficient.

E-commerce Communities: In the world of e-commerce, artificial intelligence supports product suggestions, personal shopping assistants, and community-building tools that allow users to share product reviews and insights.

AI architects vibrant digital communities, creating areas for people to interact, share, and grow. It is essential for personalizing experiences, curating material, managing communities, and encouraging interaction. As AI advances, these digital communities will become increasingly more lively and linked, providing users with a sense of belonging and a platform for meaningful interactions in the ever-expanding digital world.

Social Media Domination with AI

5.1 AI-Powered Social Media Strategies: Transforming Engagement in the Digital Era

S taying ahead of the curve in the fast-paced and ever-changing world of social media is a daunting undertaking. Businesses and content creators require a competitive advantage in an age when millions of postings, tweets, and videos compete for attention every second. AI has emerged as the secret weapon that supercharges social media tactics, transforming how people connect, interact, and communicate in the digital age.

The Revolution of Social Media

People assemble, connect, and share their opinions, experiences, and preferences on social media platforms, which have evolved into the modern town square. They've changed how businesses and individuals interact, providing unparalleled reach and viral exposure. However, as the social media landscape evolves, efficiently catching and holding the audience's attention has become a complicated art.

Artificial Intelligence as a Catalyst

AI serves as a catalyst, propelling social media initiatives into the future. It provides many tools and approaches to improve every part of a social media strategy. Here's how AI boosts these strategies:

1. **Content Personalization:** To deliver personalized content, AI analyzes user data such as behaviour, preferences, and engagement history. For example, social media sites utilize AI to prioritize information in users' feeds, ensuring they get postings from their most engaged friends, pages, or groups.

2. **Content Curation and Recommendation**: Artificial intelligence can help with content curation and recommendation. Based on user interactions and input, it recommends articles, videos, products, and advertisements. This guarantees that visitors only see material directly related to their interests.

3. **Chatbots and Virtual Assistants:** Chatbots and virtual assistants improve user engagement by answering questions, delivering information, and engaging in casual conversation. They give instant support and foster community in the digital sphere.

4. **Data Analysis**: AI is a data analysis master. It can process massive amounts of data in real time, providing insights into user behaviour and patterns. Businesses can make informed decisions, fine-tune their content, and alter their strategy on the go, thanks to this data-driven approach.

5. **Advertising and Targeting**: Artificial intelligence enables modern advertising algorithms for exact targeting. Advertisers can utilize laser-focused communications to reach their ideal audience, enhancing ad efficiency and return on investment.

Applications on Social Media Platforms

The impact of AI can be seen across multiple social media platforms:

Facebook: AI is used by Facebook for content recommendation, ad targeting, and content control. It assists users in discovering relevant material and ensures that advertisements reach the intended audience.

Twitter: Twitter utilizes AI to filter spam, detect false accounts, and promote content. By promoting accurate content and connections, it improves the entire user experience.

Instagram's AI-powered algorithm tailors the material in users' feeds depending on their interactions and preferences. It ensures that users interact with the most exciting and relevant posts.

LinkedIn uses AI for job recommendations, content recommendations, and targeted advertising. It assists professionals in connecting, networking, and discovering new opportunities.

AI-Enhanced Social Media Strategies in the Future

The future of AI-enhanced social media strategies seems bright. As AI technology advances, it will grow better at understanding user intent, providing more tailored experiences, and providing proactive answers. The social media ecosystem will continue to expand, with new opportunities to connect, engage, and communicate emerging.

Artificial intelligence is the driving force behind supercharging social media campaigns. It improves personalization, curation, and information recommendation, enables chatbots and virtual assistants, provides data-driven insights, and optimizes advertising. As AI advances, social media strategies will become more dynamic and engaging, giving businesses and content providers a competitive advantage in the ever-changing digital era.

5.2 Artificial Intelligence for Content Optimization and Scheduling: Increasing Digital Engagement

Staying current and connecting with your audience is a constant challenge in today's fast-paced, content-driven digital market. Information creators, businesses, and marketers always seek innovative methods to connect to their target audience with intriguing, timely information. Artificial intelligence (AI) has emerged as a potent ally in this endeavour, capable of optimizing content and scheduling its distribution for optimum impact.

AI's Influence on Content Optimization

Content optimization entails adapting content to an audience's needs, preferences, and expectations. AI plays an integral part in this process by providing the following advantages:

Audience Segmentation: AI can examine large datasets to discover discrete audience segments. Understanding these groups allows content providers to tailor their messaging to specific audiences.

Personalization: To personalize content, AI-driven algorithms can assess user behaviour and preferences. Individuals will receive content that is most relevant to them, enhancing user engagement and happiness.

Content Recommendations: AI can make content suggestions based on the user's history and preferences. Streaming platforms like Netflix and music services like Spotify, for example, employ AI to recommend movies, music, and other content based on individual tastes.

A/B Testing of Content: AI can assist content creators in doing A/B testing to determine which versions of material perform best. This ensures that the material is optimized for the most significant possible impact.

SEO Optimization: Artificial intelligence-powered solutions can optimize content for search engines. They examine term trends, user search behaviour, and industry competitiveness to make content recommendations that improve search engine ranks.

Artificial Intelligence for Content Scheduling and Distribution

Effective content scheduling is required to guarantee that material reaches the appropriate audience at the appropriate time. AI improves content dissemination in a variety of ways:

Optimal Posting Times: Artificial intelligence can assess user behaviour trends and recommend the best times to submit material. This increases the likelihood that posts will be viewed and engaged.

Cross-Platform Synchronization: Artificial intelligence solutions can synchronize content delivery across many channels, assuring consistent messaging and branding. This multi-channel strategy extends the reach and effect of the material.

Automated Posting: AI can automate content scheduling and posting, decreasing the need for manual involvement and ensuring that information is published at the most appropriate times.

AI-powered chatbots and virtual assistants can interact with users in real time, answering questions and providing support anytime they interact with the material. This enhances the user experience and increases engagement.

Applications in a Variety of Industries

AI-powered content optimization and scheduling have numerous uses in a variety of industries:

Marketing: Artificial intelligence (AI) assists marketers in tailoring content to specific audiences, optimizing email campaigns, and scheduling social media postings for optimum interaction.

Publishing firms utilize AI to optimize headlines, tag material for search engine optimization, and schedule content distribution based on audience preferences.

E-commerce platforms use artificial intelligence to personalize product recommendations, improve website content for search engines, and plan email marketing campaigns.

News and Media: AI is used by news providers for content recommendations and personalized news feeds. AI also assists in the timing of content publication to match with peak audience engagement.

Individual bloggers and content creators employ AI-powered solutions to optimize blog posts, boost search engine rankings, and plan content publishing.

Artificial intelligence has become a vital tool for content optimization and scheduling, improving content relevance, personalization, and dissemination. As artificial intelligence (AI) technology evolves, it is poised to reshape how content creators and businesses interact with their audiences, ensuring that the appropriate content reaches the right people at the right time. This dynamic collaboration between AI and content strategy will be at the forefront of digital interaction in the following years.

5.3 The Rise of AI in Social Media Advertising: A Digital Marketing Revolution

Artificial Intelligence (AI) has emerged as the kingpin of success in the ever-changing world of digital marketing, where competition for customer attention is intense. It is not an exaggeration to argue that artificial intelligence has transformed social media advertising, propelling it to new levels of efficiency, precision, and effectiveness.

Social Media Advertising's Evolution

Since its start, social media advertising has come a long way. What started as simple display ads and promoted posts has become a sophisticated ecosystem of data-driven, targeted advertising. AI has been essential to this revolution, improving all aspects of social media advertising.

Audience Targeting Powered by AI

AI has dramatically enhanced the capacity to target specific audience segments. AI examines large volumes of user data using powerful algorithms to discover the most appropriate demographics for a particular ad. To guarantee that adverts reach the proper people, they can consider criteria such as age, gender, geography, hobbies, internet behaviour, and more. Before the emergence of AI, this level of audience targeting was not feasible.

Content Recommendation and Personalization

AI excels in personalization, tailoring ad material to users' preferences and actions. AI can recommend items, services, or information that are highly relevant to the individual by evaluating user data and interactions. AI makes customers feel they're being talked to directly, whether through personalized product recommendations on e-commerce platforms or content suggestions on social media.

Creating Dynamic Ads

AI is also important in ad development. It can develop ad headlines and text, for example, that are more likely to engage the target audience. AI can monitor the performance of various ad pieces in real time and optimize the content. This dynamic ad design ensures that viewers only see the most effective adverts.

Scheduling and Placement of Advertisements

AI is skilled at determining when and where to display advertisements. It can evaluate user activity to find the best times to display ads. Furthermore, AI can allocate budget resources based on the performance of multiple platforms and ad campaigns. This ensures that resources are allocated to the areas where they will have the most impact.

Analytics and Ad Performance

AI provides real-time insights regarding ad performance. Metrics like as click-through rates, conversion rates, and engagement can be tracked. Advertisers can use these insights to make data-driven decisions to optimize their ad campaigns. The power of artificial intelligence to process and evaluate massive datasets in real time is unrivalled.

Platform-Independent Applications

The impact of AI on social media advertising is platform-agnostic, encompassing multiple social media networks:

Facebook's ad platform employs artificial intelligence for audience targeting, ad delivery optimization, and ad content customization. AI-powered algorithms ensure that advertising is sent to users most likely to respond to them.

Instagram: Instagram uses AI to optimize ad placement and placement. It also employs AI to power features such as the Explore tab, which suggests content and advertisements based on user preferences.

Twitter: Twitter employs artificial intelligence for ad targeting, ensuring that individuals with relevant interests see advertising. AI can also assist advertisers in finding trending themes and hashtags.

LinkedIn: LinkedIn uses artificial intelligence (AI) for job referrals and targeted advertising. It assists professionals in connecting, networking, and discovering new opportunities.

AI and the Future of Social Media Advertising

AI is inextricably related to the future of social media advertising. AI technology will get even better at recognizing user intent, delivering personalized information, and optimizing ad campaigns as they advance. In the coming years, the marriage of AI with social media advertising will reshape the landscape of digital marketing.

Artificial intelligence has ushered in a new era of efficiency and precision in social media advertising. Its capacity to target specific audiences, tailor content, develop dynamic advertising, optimize placement, and deliver real-time performance metrics has changed the face of digital marketing. AI will continue to reign supreme in social media advertising as it evolves, ensuring businesses and marketers have the tools to engage with their target audience and achieve their marketing objectives.

IV

Monetization Strategies

Unlocking Monetization with AI

6.1 The Creator Economy's Diverse Universe of Monetization Models: Fueling Innovation and Independence

The creator economy, formerly thought to be on the outskirts, has evolved into a vibrant and varied ecosystem that allows individuals to transform their creative interests into profitable companies. The monetization options inside this digital ecosystem have increased, diversified, and paved the road for creators to reach financial independence on their terms as it continues to thrive.

The Revolution of the Creator Economy

The rise of independent creators who develop information, products, and services across numerous digital platforms characterizes the creative economy. These innovators have developed novel ways to monetize their skills, talents, and knowledge, avoiding traditional gatekeepers and forging direct connections with their audiences.

Monetization Models' Evolution

The creator economy exemplifies the vast diversity of revenue strategies available to content creators, including formats, platforms, and business models. Here are some of the most important models:

1. Sponsorships and advertising:

In-Content Advertising: Content creators finance their work by displaying advertisements, such as pre-roll and mid-roll commercials on YouTube videos or display ads on blogs and websites.

Sponsorships and Brand Collaborations: Creators collaborate with brands to market products or services to their audience naturally and accurately.

2. Memberships and Subscriptions:

Paid Subscriptions: Creators provide subscribers with premium content or perks in exchange for a recurring cost. This approach has gained popularity because of platforms such as Patreon and OnlyFans.

Creators create private online communities in which members pay for access to unique content and interactions.

3. Merchandise and E-commerce:

Digital Products: Creators sell digital products such as ebooks, courses, music, or software to their audience directly.

Physical products: Many authors sell branded products such as apparel, accessories, and collectables on platforms such as Shopify or Etsy.

4. Crowdfunding:

Crowdfunding Platforms: Crowdfunding platforms such as Kickstarter, Indiegogo, and GoFundMe are used by creators to raise funds for specific projects or creative efforts.

Tip Jars: Some platforms allow fans to leave tips or donations to help their favourite creators.

5. Affiliate Promotion:

Affiliate Links: Affiliate links allow creators to promote products or services while earning a commission on sales from their unique affiliate links.

Product Reviews: By leveraging their experience and authority in a speciality, creators provide in-depth reviews and suggestions.

6. Virtual Events & Live Streaming:

Creators conduct virtual events or live streams and sell tickets or access passes for them.

Donations & Gifts: During live streaming, viewers can donate or send virtual gifts to support the creator directly.

7. Non-fungible tokens (NFTs):

Creators tokenize digital goods such as art, music, or virtual real estate and offer them as NFTs to collectors and admirers.

8. Syndication and Licensing:

Material Licensing: Creators earn royalties by licensing their material to third parties for distribution or republishing.

Syndication: Content creators collaborate with media outlets or platforms to reach a larger audience.

The creator economy's vast universe of monetization models enables individuals to turn their interests into sustainable jobs. Creators can choose the techniques that best suit their goals and audience, whether through advertising, subscriptions, e-commerce, crowdfunding, affiliate marketing, live events, NFTs, licensing, or a combination of these. As the creative economy grows, it will be defined by innovation, independence, and an ongoing desire to reimagine what is possible in the digital era.

6.2 Personalization and Sustainability in the Age of AI-Enhanced Subscription Models

Subscription models have seen a fundamental transition in the digital age, owing to the integration of Artificial Intelligence (AI) and data-driven technologies. This combination has ushered in an era of AI-enhanced subscription models dominated by personalization, predictive analytics, and customer involvement. This innovative strategy has not only transformed how organizations distribute services and information, but it has also helped many industries establish a more sustainable and prosperous future.

Subscription Model Development

Subscription models are not new; they have been utilized for decades in various sectors. The expansion of the internet and digital platforms, on the other hand, has resulted in a paradigm shift in how these models operate. Three critical factors define the era of AI-enhanced subscription models:

Personalization based on data: AI systems analyze massive volumes of user data to produce highly personalized experiences. AI knows individual interests and habits, boosting the value of a subscription, whether it's content recommendations, product suggestions, or specialized services.

AI forecasts future user behaviour, allowing firms to anticipate demands and preferences. This allows for proactive customer service, inventory management, and content curation, ensuring that members receive what they want when they want it.

AI is continually learning and adapting, perfecting its recommendations and forecasts over time. The AI system becomes more accurate as subscribers interact with the service, creating long-term partnerships and client loyalty.

Artificial Intelligence-Enhanced Subscription Models in Action

AI integration into subscription models has been successful in a variety of industries:

1. **Streaming Services**: Platforms like Netflix and Spotify utilize artificial intelligence (AI) to propose movies, TV shows, and music, resulting in highly personalized content libraries. Users choose material that is relevant to their interests, which leads to longer membership durations.

2. **E-commerce**: AI is used by online merchants to recommend products based on a user's browsing and purchasing history. This customization boosts conversion rates and order values.

3. **Subscription Boxes**: Subscription box providers choose products based on user preferences, and artificial intelligence (AI) assists in optimizing the selection process. Customers receive boxes tailored to their preferences and needs, boosting their subscription experience.

4. **News and Media**: AI is used by media outlets to recommend articles and news topics based on individual interests. This keeps readers interested and up to date.

5. **Software as a Service (SaaS)**: AI-powered platforms provide individualized features, pricing plans, and updates. This improves the entire user experience and encourages client retention.

The era of AI-enhanced subscription models marks a massive shift in how businesses interact with customers. Subscription services may provide exceptional value to their consumers by harnessing AI's skills in data analysis, personalization, and predictive analytics. The era of AI-enhanced subscription models is defined by an unwavering commitment to improving the customer experience, increasing customer loyalty, and assuring the long-term viability and profitability of subscription-based enterprises in the digital age.

6.3 Artificial Intelligence-Powered Advertising and Sponsored Content Strategies: Transforming Digital Marketing

Artificial Intelligence (AI) has emerged as a strong force in the quickly expanding digital marketing environment, transforming how firms promote and communicate with their audiences. AI-powered advertising and sponsored content tactics have transformed how businesses communicate with their target demographics, resulting in more efficient, targeted, and impactful marketing campaigns.

The Influence of AI on Advertising

AI has become a must-have tool for modern advertisers, with a wide range of capabilities that improve every aspect of the advertising process. Here are some of the most essential aspects of AI's impact on advertising and sponsored content strategies:

1. **Targeted Marketing:**
    Target Segmentation: AI analyzes large datasets to discover different target segments, allowing advertisers to tailor their messaging for optimal relevance.
    Personalization: AI personalizes ad content based on user data and be-

haviour, ensuring that it corresponds with individual interests and generates increased engagement.

2. Ad Creatives that Change:

Ad Generation: Artificial intelligence (AI) can generate ad headlines, content, and graphic elements optimized for maximum interaction. It uses real-time performance data to optimize ad content.

A/B Testing: AI assists advertisers in testing various ad elements and determining which variations perform best. This data-driven strategy ensures that advertisements are constantly optimized.

3. Analytics Predictive:

AI forecasts user behaviour, allowing advertisers to anticipate client requirements and preferences. This allows for proactive marketing strategies and campaign modifications.

AI-powered recommendation engines propose products, services, or information based on user interactions, improving cross-selling and upselling potential.

4. Budget Allocation and Ad Placement:

AI analyzes user behaviour to discover the ideal times and platforms for ad display. This guarantees that advertisements are seen at the most effective times.

Budget Optimization: AI assigns advertising money to successful campaigns, ensuring efficient resource utilization.

5. Analytics in Real Time:

AI gives real-time information about ad performance, such as click-through rates, conversion rates, and engagement indicators. Advertisers may optimize their advertisements by making data-driven decisions.

Applications in a Variety of Industries

AI-enhanced advertising and sponsored content tactics have a wide range of applications in a variety of industries:

1. **E-commerce**: Chatbots and virtual assistants are used by online merchants to personalize product recommendations, optimize ad targeting, and improve customer experiences.

2. **Streaming Services**: Platforms like Netflix and Spotify use AI to recommend material to users, keeping them engaged and persuading them to renew their subscriptions for extended periods.

3. **Financial Services:** AI is being used by banks and investment businesses to provide targeted financial advice, tailored investment suggestions, and real-time customer support.

4. **Healthcare**: AI is used by healthcare providers to develop targeted advertisements for patient interaction, personalized health material, and telehealth services.

5. **News and Media**: AI is used in media outlets for content recommendations, personalized news feeds, and analytics on user involvement.

AI-Powered Advertising and Sponsored Content Strategies in the Future

AI-powered advertising and sponsored content techniques have a bright future. AI technology will grow more adept at interpreting user intent, creating personalized experiences, and giving proactive answers as it evolves. AI-powered advertising is likely to change the way businesses interact with their target consumers, making campaigns more efficient, relevant, and impactful.

Artificial intelligence has changed the advertising and sponsored content environment, ushering in a new era of efficiency and personalization. This dynamic marketing technique enables organizations to connect with their audiences in previously imagined ways. AI-powered advertising and sponsored content initiatives are reshaping how businesses interact with their customers and prospects, laying the groundwork for the future of digital marketing.

E-Commerce and AI-Powered Sales

7.1 The Marriage of AI and E-Commerce: A Revolution in Online Shopping

T he marriage of Artificial Intelligence (AI) with e-commerce has created a new era of online buying, where tailored experiences, intelligent recommendations, and data-driven strategies are the standard. This dynamic collaboration is changing the way customers find products, make purchasing decisions, and interact with brands while also enabling businesses to prosper in the competitive e-commerce landscape.

E-Commerce's Evolution

E-commerce, or the buying and selling of goods and services over the internet, has progressed from simple online catalogues to the sophisticated, data-driven marketplace that it is today. The incorporation of AI into this ecosystem has been critical in revolutionizing e-commerce, providing several significant benefits:

Personalization: AI analyzes massive volumes of user data to learn about people's tastes, activities, and purchasing habits. This allows e-commerce platforms to give individualized product recommendations and user experiences, making it easier for customers to find what they want.

AI-driven predictive analytics estimate consumer behaviour, allowing businesses to anticipate client wants and customize marketing efforts. These insights provide a competitive advantage in everything from inventory management to pricing optimization.

Customer Service: AI-powered chatbots and virtual assistants give rapid assistance, answer inquiries, and recommend products. In the digital domain, this improves customer support and develops a sense of community.

Inventory & Supply Chain Management: Artificial intelligence optimizes inventory levels and simplifies supply chain procedures, ensuring that products are readily available and efficiently supplied.

AI's Role in E-Commerce

Product Recommendations: AI algorithms examine user behaviour and historical data to recommend products or services based on personal preferences. Amazon and other platforms have set the bar for these intelligent recommendations.

Visual Search: Artificial intelligence allows users to search for products using visuals. AI can find comparable items in e-commerce catalogues by evaluating images, simplifying the search process.

Price Optimization: Artificial intelligence analyzes market data, competitive pricing, and consumer behaviour to establish ideal product prices that maximize profits and sales.

Virtual Fitting Rooms: AI-powered virtual fitting rooms enable buyers to try on apparel and accessories digitally, improving the online shopping experience and decreasing returns.

Chatbots and Customer Service: Artificial intelligence-powered chatbots and virtual assistants give rapid assistance, answer questions, and lead customers through the purchasing process.

Applications in a Variety of Industries

The convergence of AI and e-commerce goes beyond traditional retail:

Food and Grocery Delivery: For food delivery and grocery e-commerce platforms, AI is utilized to optimize delivery routes, estimate demand, and ensure effective order fulfilment.

Travel and Hospitality: AI enables recommendation engines for booking flights, lodgings, and travel experiences. Chatbots answer client questions and offer travel advice.

Healthcare and Telemedicine: AI is used in healthcare and telemedicine e-commerce platforms to facilitate online consultations, appointment scheduling, and pharmaceutical delivery.

Automotive: Artificial intelligence (AI) assists customers in browsing, customizing, and purchasing vehicles online, as well as scheduling test drives and maintenance services.

Subscription Services: AI is used in subscription-based e-commerce models to personalize product selections, forecast subscriber preferences, and improve user experience.

E-Commerce Using AI in the Future

The future of AI-enhanced e-commerce is bright. As artificial intelligence (AI) technology evolves, it will continue to create more personalized and efficient shopping experiences, redefine customer involvement, and propel the e-commerce industry toward more significant innovation.

The convergence of AI with e-commerce is a disruptive force that has reshaped how consumers shop online, and businesses operate. This convergence of technology and commerce is characterized by personalization, predictive analytics, and improved customer service. AI promises to create more sophisticated and intelligent e-commerce experiences as it evolves, ensuring that the online buying journey remains fun, efficient, and user-centric.

7.2 Personalization and AI-Driven Product Recommendations: The Future of Customer Engagement

Personalization and AI-driven product recommendations have become the backbone of generating unique, bespoke purchasing experiences for consumers in the age of digital commerce. This dynamic combination of technology and data analysis not only encourages customer engagement but also has a substantial impact on the success and profitability of e-commerce firms.

Customer Engagement's Evolution

Customer interaction has progressed from a one-size-fits-all model to a highly tailored, data-driven experience. This movement is being accelerated by incorporating Artificial Intelligence (AI) into e-commerce platforms, which allows businesses to offer levels of customization previously thought unfeasible.

The Role of AI in Personalization and Product Recommendations

Data Analysis: AI systems examine massive amounts of client data, including browsing history, purchase behaviour, demographics, and real-time interactions. This information serves as the foundation for individualized recommendations.

AI predicts client behaviour, allowing firms to anticipate requirements and preferences. These forecasts are then utilized to recommend appropriate items, promotions, and content.

AI-powered recommendation engines utilize machine learning techniques to deliver individualized product recommendations. These algorithms continually adapt to client interactions, learning from each click and purchase to fine-tune recommendations.

Personalization of content: AI personalizes content such as marketing emails and website content to match individual tastes and browsing history. This not only boosts engagement but also conversions.

Key AI-Driven Personalization and Recommendations Components

Product Suggestions: AI systems evaluate customer data to recommend products that match individual tastes. This tailored strategy can enhance the likelihood of a purchase and increase average order values dramatically.

Email Marketing: AI improves email marketing by segmenting clients based on their behaviour and preferences, resulting in highly relevant email content. This results in increased open and click-through rates.

AI may change prices in real time based on supply and demand, customer behaviour, and rival pricing. This dynamic pricing model increases earnings while also satisfying customers.

AI enables visual search, allowing users to find products by submitting photographs. The system recognizes comparable items in the product catalogue, which speeds up the search process.

Chatbots and Virtual Assistants: AI-powered chatbots offer instant assistance, answer inquiries, and aid clients in navigating e-commerce platforms. Virtual assistants provide personal product recommendations and shopping assistance.

Applications Across Industries

Personalization powered by AI has an impact that reaches beyond e-commerce:

Streaming Services: Platforms like Netflix and Spotify employ artificial intelligence to recommend movies, music, and other content to keep users engaged and subscribed.

Food delivery apps use AI to recommend restaurants and foods based on user preferences, improving the ordering process.

Travel and Hospitality: AI-powered recommendation engines let passengers plan customized rooms, flights, and activities.

Healthcare and Telemedicine: AI enables personalized health and wellness suggestions, providing individualized counsel and guidance.

Automotive: AI-powered personalization improves the automobile purchasing experience by allowing buyers to browse and configure their dream vehicle online.

Personalization and AI-driven product recommendations constitute a significant improvement in consumer interaction, transforming how businesses connect with their customers. The power of AI enables businesses to provide personalized shopping experiences that increase customer pleasure and loyalty. As AI advances, the future of personalization promises to be even more engaging and dynamic, ensuring that customers receive the content and goods they want when they need them.

7.3 Chatbots as Sales and Customer Service Engines: Transforming Customer Experiences

Chatbots have evolved as vital tools in customer care and sales, combining artificial intelligence (AI) with real-time interactions. These AI-powered bots are formidable forces, improving customer service and driving sales while altering how businesses interact with customers.

Customer Service and Sales Evolution

In reaction to shifting consumer behaviour, customer service and sales tactics have developed. The advent of digital and e-commerce platforms has raised expectations for firms to provide quick, efficient, and personalized encounters. Chatbots have played an essential role in this progress, changing customer experiences.

Chatbots' Role in Customer Support and Sales

Chatbots can respond to frequent consumer requests by offering information about products, services, or general corporate information.

Order Processing: Bots streamline the purchase process by assisting with order placement, tracking, and returns.

Chatbots are used to plan appointments and manage reservations in various industries.

Product Recommendations: Chatbots evaluate client data to recommend products or services that match individual tastes, enhancing sales prospects.

Troubleshooting: Bots can walk customers through troubleshooting procedures, providing step-by-step directions for problem resolution.

Follow-Up Communication: Chatbots provide post-interaction follow-up to ensure that consumers are satisfied and to address any outstanding issues.

Key Chatbot Powerhouse Components

Chatbots run around the clock, answering client questions and sales chores. They are invaluable when it comes to serving worldwide audiences and time zones.

Chatbots respond quickly, minimizing wait times and enhancing customer happiness. They can handle several consumer requests without becoming fatigued.

Personalization: Artificial intelligence-powered chatbots evaluate user data to adapt responses and recommendations to individual preferences, resulting in a more engaging and relevant customer experience.

Chatbots provide consistent and accurate responses, reducing human errors and ensuring customers receive consistent information.

Scalability: Businesses may scale their chatbot operations to meet increasing demand, making them suitable for small and large corporations.

Applications in a Variety of Industries

E-commerce: Chatbots are used by online merchants to provide product information, purchase assistance, and order tracking and returns.

Travel and hospitality: Chatbots are used by travel companies and hotels to book reservations, answer travel-related issues, and give guest service.

Healthcare: Medical facilities use chatbots to schedule appointments, answer health questions, and provide primary medical advice.

Banking and finance: Chatbots are used by financial institutions for account queries, transaction support, and financial advising.

Education: Chatbots are used at educational institutions for enrollment assistance, course information, and general student support.

Chatbots' Potential as Sales and Customer Support Engines

With continual technical developments, the future of chatbots seems bright. Chatbots will grow smarter as AI and natural language processing improve, recognizing user intent and engaging in more intricate conversations. They will continue to innovate and improve customer experiences to generate sales.

Chatbots are revolutionizing customer assistance and sales by providing a dynamic, efficient, and personalized approach to interaction. These AI-powered behemoths reduce customer questions, increase sales, and improve the customer experience. Chatbots will continue to be crucial tools for organizations in the digital age, providing outstanding customer assistance and increasing sales.

V

Entrepreneurship and Business Development

Initiating Your AI-Infused Startup

8.1 Thriving in a Technological Revolution: Navigating the Startup Landscape in 2024

The startup scene in 2024 will be a dynamic and ever-changing ecosystem with tremendous opportunities and challenges. As technology advances astoundingly, entrepreneurs and startups enter a revolutionary era in which innovation, adaptability, and a clear awareness of new trends are critical to success.

Startups in the Present Situation

To effectively navigate the startup market, it is critical first to examine the existing situation of startups in the present. Several significant factors define this landscape:

Technology Disruption: The rapid pace of technology innovation is altering sectors everywhere. Artificial intelligence, blockchain, augmented reality, and other emerging technologies are opening up new possibilities and posing new challenges to existing business structures.

Access to Capital: Access to capital is still critical for startups. While venture capital, angel investors, and crowdfunding sites provide financial assistance, investment competition is fierce.

Workplace Collaboration and Remote Work: The COVID-19 pandemic has irreversibly impacted work dynamics. Remote work, digital communication tools, and a scattered workforce are becoming the norm, presenting companies with benefits and challenges.

Sustainability and Social Effect: Sustainability and social effect are becoming increasingly crucial to startups. Both investors and customers are demanding ethical and environmentally responsible behaviour.

Success Strategies for 2024 and Beyond

Embrace Technological Advancements: It is critical to stay current on developing technologies and their applications. Startups that use artificial intelligence, blockchain, and other advancements have a competitive advantage.

Solve Real-World Issues: Identify significant issues and offer creative solutions. Startups that address actual pain areas and needs have a better chance of success.

Remote Work and Digital Collaboration: Accept remote work and efficiently employ digital collaboration technologies. This allows you to access a worldwide talent pool while also streamlining operations.

Integrate sustainability and social responsibility into your company concept. To attract aware consumers, consider eco-friendly methods, ethical sourcing, and social impact activities.

Adaptability: The ability to quickly pivot and adjust is priceless. The business landscape is volatile, and firms that can pivot quickly are more likely to survive and grow.

Customer-Centric Approach: Put customer feedback and requirements first. A customer-centric strategy ensures that your product or service is well-received by your target market.

Diversify your financing sources as part of your funding strategy. To assure financial stability, investigate venture capital, angel investors, crowdfunding, grants, and bootstrapping.

Challenges and Considerations

Despite the opportunities, companies will confront considerable hurdles in 2024 and beyond:

The startup landscape is fiercely competitive, with many competitors vying for attention and money.

Evolving rules in data privacy, cryptocurrencies, and digital commerce might impact startup operations.

Cybersecurity: As businesses become more digital, startups must emphasize cybersecurity to protect their operations and customer data.

Attracting and maintaining top personnel is difficult, especially in the tech sector, where skilled experts are in high demand.

Economic Uncertainty: Global economic conditions can impact startup funding and consumer buying habits.

The startup ecosystem in 2024 will provide limitless potential for entrepreneurs who can skillfully traverse its intricacies. Startups may prosper despite the continuous technological transformation and contribute to defining the future of business and society by embracing technical breakthroughs, remaining customer-centric, and adjusting to new trends.

8.2 AI Startup Funding Horizons: Navigating the Investment Landscape

Securing investment is a vital and revolutionary growth stage in the ever-changing world of artificial intelligence (AI) enterprises. With the potential to disrupt various industries, artificial intelligence (AI) creates massive opportunities for entrepreneurs. Navigating the fundraising market for AI businesses, on the other hand, requires knowing the many sources of capital and adjusting tactics to the sector's particular difficulties and potential.

AI as an Innovation Catalyst

AI has emerged as a critical driver of innovation in various industries. Integrating AI technology transforms the business landscape, from healthcare and finance to e-commerce and driverless vehicles. As a result, AI firms are not only on the cutting edge of transformation but also generating significant investor attention.

Funding Horizons: Capital Sources for AI Startups

AI companies have access to a variety of funding sources, each with its own set of characteristics and requirements. These financing horizons are classified as follows:

Bootstrapping: Many AI entrepreneurs start with their own money, personal investments, or royalties from early product sales. Bootstrapping allows for independence but limits the size of operations.

Angel investors assist firms with early-stage investment in exchange for stock or convertible debt. They frequently bring industry knowledge and connections to the table.

Venture Capital (VC): businesses invest in AI startups in exchange for shares, intending to profit significantly. AI-focused venture capital firms are especially interested in supporting businesses in this industry.

Corporate Venture Capital: Many large corporations have their venture capital divisions. These corporate venture funds make investments in businesses that match their strategic objectives.

Crowdfunding platforms enable entrepreneurs to raise capital from a vast number of people. This method is especially effective for creating interest and support from many people.

Government Grants and Subsidies: Many governments worldwide provide grants, subsidies, and tax breaks to stimulate AI research and development. These can be critical sources of funding for early-stage enterprises.

In exchange for equity, accelerators and incubators give entrepreneurs guidance, resources, and cash. They frequently conclude on a demo day, during which businesses pitch to investors.

Tokens and Initial Coin Offerings (ICOs): Some AI businesses, particularly those involved in blockchain and cryptocurrency initiatives, acquire funds through ICOs by issuing tokens to investors.

Strategic alliances and corporate collaborations: AI startups can form alliances with more giant corporations to access resources, distribution channels, and expertise. These collaborations may include equity investments.

Debt Financing: AI startups can obtain loans or lines of credit to fund their operations by pledging assets or predicted revenue as collateral.

Funding prospects for AI businesses provide a variety of alternatives for entrepreneurs wishing to capitalize on the potential of AI technologies. To successfully traverse this ecosystem, businesses must carefully assess the sources of finance that most correspond with their ambitions, as well as be prepared to meet the unique problems and issues connected with the AI sector. AI companies may acquire the capital they need to advance innovation and bring their products to market with the appropriate strategy and a compelling value offer.

Innovations in the Creative Arts and AI Synergy

9.1 Artificial Intelligence Renaissance in Art and Design: A Creative Revolution

The convergence of artificial intelligence (AI) and the domains of art and design has spawned a modern renaissance in which innovation, creativity, and human-machine collaboration are changing the boundaries of artistic expression and design. This modern fusion of technology and artistic vision is ushering in a transformative period in visual and creative arts.

AI as a Catalyst for Creativity

AI has sparked a renaissance in art and design by allowing artists and designers to leverage its potential in a variety of ways:

Generative Art: AI algorithms may develop artworks independently or in conjunction with human artists, allowing them to experiment with new forms, styles, and concepts.

Enhanced Creativity: AI technologies enable artists to quickly experiment with new ideas, styles, and approaches, enabling limitless creativity.

Design Automation: AI-powered design tools automate time-consuming and repetitive activities, allowing designers to focus on creativity and innovation.

AI analyzes data and user behaviour to predict trends and preferences, providing insights that impact artistic and design decisions.

Personalization: AI-powered solutions enable personalized art and design experiences by adapting creations to individual tastes.

Creative Assistance: AI-powered technologies advise artists and designers, such as colours, compositions, and styles.

Key Art and Design Transformations

The revival of AI in art and design has resulted in significant changes:

Artistic Collaboration: AI is increasingly being viewed as a creative partner, with artists partnering with AI systems to create one-of-a-kind pieces.

NFT (Non-Fungible Token) marketplaces have grown in popularity, allowing artists to sell digital work as unique, verifiable assets.

Augmented and Virtual Reality: AR and VR technology enable interactive and immersive artistic encounters, pushing traditional art to new heights.

Design Automation: AI-driven automation is easing the creative process in graphic design, web design, and interior design.

Data Visualization: Artificial intelligence (AI) assists in developing data-driven art, making complex data more accessible and exciting.

AI can optimize architecture designs for energy efficiency, aesthetics, and structural integrity.

Applications in a Variety of Art Forms

AI has a significant impact on painting, sculpture, and digital art. Artists and AI algorithms are collaborating to create spectacular visual masterpieces.

AI generates compositions, produces music, and improves sound engineering. AI-powered music and sound design are pioneering new territory.

Fashion & Apparel: AI is applied in fashion design, fashion trend prediction, and creating sustainable and personalized clothes.

Film and Animation: Artificial intelligence (AI) aids in film editing, animation, and visual effects, lowering production costs and increasing creativity.

AI assists designers in optimizing product designs for utility, attractiveness, and cost-efficiency.

The resurgence of AI in art and design demonstrates the boundless possibilities that emerge when creativity meets technology. Human-AI collaboration is altering artistic expression, design, and creativity, and as AI evolves, we may anticipate an era of extraordinary artistic exploration and invention, further transforming the creative environment.

9.2 Navigating the Creative Horizon in the AI Era: An Innovation and Imagination Journey

The AI era has heralded a new era of creation, providing artists, creators, and innovators with a large canvas to explore and reinvent what is possible. As artificial intelligence (AI) becomes more incorporated into the creative process, the creative horizon broadens, revealing a landscape of options that combines human genius and technical innovation.

The AI-Enhanced Creative Process

Incorporating AI into the creative process has cleared the way for transformative developments in various fields, including music, visual arts, literature, design, and others. This merger of human creativity and AI-driven capabilities is significantly changing the creative horizon:

Augmented Creativity: AI provides artists and creators with a toolset of inventive resources, allowing them to experiment with new styles and forms, as well as explore new concepts.

Efficiency & Automation: AI automates repetitive processes in the creative process, allowing creators to focus on creativity, invention, and experimentation.

Collaboration between AI experts, technologists, and creative workers leads to a cross-pollination of ideas and knowledge, creating a fertile environment for new ventures.

Personalization: AI tailors creative outputs to individual interests, ensuring that art, music, and content appeal to a wide range of people.

Data-Driven Creativity: Artificial intelligence (AI) uses data to provide insights into trends, audience behaviour, and creative potential, influencing creative activities.

Immersive Experiences: Artificial intelligence (AI) - powered technologies such as augmented reality (AR) and virtual reality (VR) produce immersive artistic experiences that blur the lines between the virtual and actual worlds.

Innovations in a Variety of Creative Domains

AI-driven creativity has an impact on a wide range of creative fields:

AI-Generated Music: Artificial intelligence-generated compositions, real-time music accompaniment, and music enhancement technologies transform how music is made and experienced.

AI-powered algorithms engage with human artists to produce new types of visual art, experimenting with new styles and approaches.

Text, poetry, and literature are generated by AI, revolutionizing the world of creative writing and narrative.

Graphic and web design: AI automates graphic design chores, web layout generation, and user interface design to streamline design processes.

Film and Animation: Artificial intelligence (AI) aids with video editing, special effects, animation, and even scriptwriting, extending the boundaries of visual narrative.

Fashion & Apparel: AI anticipates fashion trends, simplifies clothes design, and promotes environmentally friendly fashion practices.

In the AI era, the future of creation is distinguished by boundless possibilities. As AI evolves and adapts, it will challenge creators to go outside their current creative constraints and explore new levels of human-machine collaboration. The creative horizon will continue to be shaped by innovations, problems, and ethical considerations.

Traversing the creative horizon in the AI era requires invention, imagination, and investigation. The collaborative collaboration between human creativity and AI technology is defining the future of creative expression, opening up new vistas of artistic possibilities and pushing the limits of what is possible in creativity and innovation.

VI

Future-Proofing Your Creator Economy Career

The Future Unveiled: AI Trends and Beyond

10.1 Glimpsing into AI Trends for 2024 and Beyond The Future of Artificial Intelligence

Artificial intelligence (AI) constantly evolves, with innovations and profound advancements. As we look ahead to 2024 and beyond, the AI environment is set to alter dramatically, providing a view into the technology developments, societal effects, and emerging trends that will shape our AI-driven future.

1. Responsible AI Development and Ethical AI

The ethical issues surrounding AI are becoming more prominent. AI system development will progressively prioritize ethical principles and responsibility in 2024. Addressing prejudice in AI systems, maintaining openness, and protecting privacy and security are all part of this. Building trust in AI technologies will need ethical AI practices.

2. Artificial Intelligence in Healthcare and Life Sciences

The impact of AI on healthcare is quickly growing. AI-powered diagnostics, drug discovery, and individualized treatment regimens will improve sophistication and accessibility. AI will not only accelerate medical research but will also enable individuals to take control of their health through AI-powered health monitoring and wearable gadgets.

3. Artificial intelligence in education and skill development

AI is reshaping the educational landscape. Personalized learning powered by AI, intelligent tutoring systems, and educational chatbots will provide specialized learning experiences. As education becomes more data-driven, artificial intelligence (AI) will improve student outcomes and lifelong skill development.

4. Artificial Intelligence and Climate Change Mitigation

AI is poised to become a critical weapon in the fight against climate change. AI's contributions to sustainability and environmental preservation will be increasingly visible, from minimizing energy consumption to enhancing weather forecasting. AI will also enable the development of more environmentally friendly and efficient technology.

5. Artificial Intelligence in Financial Services

AI will transform the banking sector, notably in fraud detection, risk assess-ment, and customer service. Financial institutions may use AI's predictive powers to make data-driven decisions and provide more tailored services while preventing financial crimes.

6. Augmented Reality (AR) / Virtual Reality (VR) with AI

AI will substantially improve AR and VR experiences. Immersive environments for gaming, education, training, and entertainment will be created using AI-driven content production, object identification, and spatial tracking. The combination of AI and AR/VR will change the way we interact with both digital and physical settings.

7. Artificial Intelligence in Content Creation and Generation

AI will continue revolutionizing content creation in various forms, including written content, visual art, and music. AI-generated content will become more widespread, generating disputes over authenticity and authorship. AI-powered content will also cater to individual interests, providing consumers a more personalized experience.

8. AI-Advanced Cybersecurity

AI-driven solutions will become increasingly important in the fight against cyber threats. The ability of artificial intelligence (AI) to recognize anomalies and patterns in real-time will strengthen cybersecurity measures, protecting sensitive data and digital infrastructure against emerging threats.

9. AI and Quantum Computing

The convergence of quantum computing and artificial intelligence will open up new possibilities. Quantum computers will handle complex AI problems at previously unheard-of speeds and accuracy, transforming sectors like medicine development, cryptography, and climate prediction.

10. Collaboration between humans and artificial intelligence

Human-AI collaboration will become more natural and seamless. AI-powered chatbots, virtual assistants, and human-AI teams will collaborate on complicated tasks, opening new avenues for productivity and problem-solving across industries.

11. Artificial Intelligence in Governance and Policy

The impact of AI on governance and policymaking will grow. To address social concerns and establish informed policies, governments will use AI for data analysis, decision assistance, and predictive analytics.

The AI landscape for 2024 and beyond is dynamic, offering industry-wide innovation and revolution. With ethical AI at the forefront, AI's involvement in healthcare, education, sustainability, content production, and other areas will enable individuals, businesses, and societies to fully realize the potential of AI while ethically tackling its issues. As AI advances, it will provide unparalleled potential to affect our future in significant ways.

10.2 Navigating the Ethical Landscape of AI: A Journey to Responsible Artificial Intelligence

As AI technologies continue to affect our communities, industries, and daily lives, ethical concerns about artificial intelligence (AI) have taken centre stage. Navigating the ethical terrain of AI has become an urgent task, driven by the need to guarantee that AI is developed, deployed, and utilized responsibly and accountable. This extensive investigation digs into the many ethical dimensions of AI, guiding us through the intricacies and problems of this ever-changing sector.

AI's Ethical Implications

As AI technologies advance, the ethical imperative becomes more apparent. Addressing these ethical considerations is critical for building public trust, safeguarding individual rights, and avoiding unexpected effects. The following ethical pillars highlight the importance of navigating the AI ethical landscape:

Transparency and Accountability: Fundamental ethical standards include ensuring transparency in AI algorithms and decision-making processes, as well as holding developers and users accountable for their AI systems.

Transparency generates trust, and accountability encourages responsible use.

Fairness and Bias Mitigation: AI systems must be built and executed to be fair and devoid of bias. Bias is a critical ethical concern since it can perpetuate discrimination and inequities.

Protection of personal data and respect for individuals' privacy rights are non-negotiable ethical factors in AI. It is critical to protect sensitive information and limit data exposure.

Safety and security: It is critical to ensure the safety of AI systems, particularly in applications such as autonomous vehicles and healthcare. AI security measures must protect against malicious use and system flaws.

Human Autonomy and Control: It is critical to maintain human autonomy and control over AI systems. AI should supplement rather than replace human decision-making, and users must have the last word.

Accountable Governance and Regulations: Policymakers and regulatory organizations are critical in establishing the ethical framework for artificial intelligence development and deployment. Responsible AI regulations must be developed and enforced.

The Difficulties of Navigating the Ethical AI Landscape

The ethical landscape of artificial intelligence is laden with issues and considerations that necessitate sophisticated approaches:

Bias Mitigation: Due to the biases ingrained in training data, addressing bias in AI systems is complicated. Developers must use strategies to reduce bias and assure fairness.

Ethical Decision-Making: AI systems frequently make judgments that impact individuals, creating issues of moral agency and responsibility. Creating AI systems that can make ethical decisions is a new study area.

Data Privacy: A continuing difficulty is balancing the need for data to train AI systems with privacy rights and data protection. It is critical to strike the proper balance.

Emerging Technologies: As artificial intelligence advances, ethical issues arise, such as deepfakes, synthetic media, and autonomous weaponry. These technologies necessitate the establishment of ethical frameworks and legislation.

Ethical AI in Global Contexts: Because AI ethics differ between cultures and countries, a universal knowledge of ethical AI concepts that respect local nuances is required.

Accountability and Responsibility

Navigating the ethical landscape of AI starts with responsibility and accountability. AI developers, companies, and governments all have responsibilities for ensuring that AI is used ethically. This responsibility includes:

Developers and Organizations: AI designers and deployment must consider ethics, proactively addressing prejudice, justice, transparency, and safety.

Governments and Policymakers: Governments play a critical role in developing and implementing AI ethical rules, guaranteeing compliance and responsibility.

Users and Society: Individuals and society must be educated about ethical AI practices and advocate for responsible development and use.

The Path Forward in Ethical AI

The path through the ethical environment of artificial intelligence is a dynamic one, distinguished by continual difficulties and evolutions. As AI continues to have an impact on our world, the ethical framework that surrounds it must adapt and grow. Ethical AI development is a commitment to responsible innovation, and its success is critical to realizing AI's revolutionary promise while safeguarding human rights and values.

Understanding the ethical terrain of AI is a collaborative effort involving individuals, organizations, and legislators. We can construct a road to responsible AI development and usage by addressing transparency, fairness, privacy, safety, and other ethical concerns. By doing so, we may realize AI's full potential while ensuring it adheres to our shared values and ethical norms.

10.3 Embracing Continuous Learning and Adaptation: The Keys to Succeeding in a Rapidly Changing World

In today's fast-paced and ever-changing world, the capacity to adapt and learn on the fly is not just a valued skill; it is also a requirement for personal and professional development. The constant pace of change, fueled by technology, globalization, and societal transformations, necessitates that individuals and organizations make learning and adaptability an essential component of their DNA. This in-depth investigation digs into the relevance of embracing continuous learning and adaptation, providing insights into why it is necessary, the problems it provides, and the techniques for prospering in this dynamic world.

The Need for Continuous Learning and Adaptation

Technological Advancement: Rapid technological growth affects sectors and job markets, necessitating new skills and knowledge.

Globalization: A connected world necessitates cross-cultural competency and the capacity to function in various settings.

Solving Complex Problems: The issues we confront are becoming more complex, necessitating adaptation and the ability to learn quickly.

Changing Careers: People no longer have a single career for the rest of their lives. When changing careers, it is critical to continue learning.

Life-Long Learning: Education is only the beginning of learning. Lifelong learning is essential for personal growth and professional success.

Challenges in Embracing Continuous Learning and Adaptation

- While the advantages of continual learning and adaptation are apparent, there are certain obstacles to overcome:

- **Time Constraints:** It might be challenging to balance learning with work, family, and other commitments.

- **Access to Educational Resources and Opportunities:** Some individuals and communities may have restricted access to educational resources and opportunities.

- People may resist change because they perceive it to be disruptive and uncomfortable.

- **Overwhelming Information:** Sorting through massive volumes of information can be overwhelming.

Embracing Continuous Learning and Adaptation Strategies

- **Growth Mindset:** Cultivate a growth mentality where setbacks are viewed as chances to learn and adapt.

- **Set Specific Goals:** Define your learning objectives and set specific, attainable goals.

- **Structured Learning:** Select formal or informal learning techniques based on your learning style and requirements.

- **Technology Adaptation:** Use technology for online courses, webinars, and digital materials.

- **Collaboration and networking:** Collaborate with peers, mentors, and experts to acquire insights and assistance.

- **Reflect and Apply:** Reflect on what you've learned regularly and apply it to real-life situations.

- **Stay Curious:** Develop curiosity as a motivator for lifelong learning and exploration.

- **Resilience:** Accept setbacks and disappointments as learning opportunities and grow resilience.

Organizational Continuous Learning

- **Employee Training and Development:** Invest in employee training and development initiatives.

- **Mentorship and Coaching:** To enhance learning, provide chances for mentorship and coaching.

- **Innovation:** Encourage staff to participate in innovation and creative problem-solving.

- **Platforms for Knowledge Sharing and Collaborative Learning:** Create platforms for knowledge sharing and collaborative learning.

- **Flexibility:** Allow staff to adjust to new jobs and responsibilities by being flexible and open to change.

The Advantages of Continuous Learning and Adaptation

- **Personal Development**: Better skills, knowledge, and personal development.

- **Career Advancement**: Increased employability and career opportunities.

- **Problem-Solving**: Increased adaptability and problem-solving abilities.

- **Innovation**: The capability to drive innovation and constructive change.

- **Resilience**: Increased resilience in the face of difficulties and uncertainties.

The Path to Thriving in a Dynamic World

Accepting constant learning and adaptation is a dynamic process that leads to personal and professional development. It enables individuals and organizations to flourish in a constantly changing world while also contributing to the creativity and progress that characterize the twenty-first century. Continuous learning is not a destination; it is a way of life that ensures preparation for future challenges and opportunities. In a world marked by change, people who embrace learning as a lifelong quest are best prepared to negotiate the modern age's rugged terrain.

200+ Proven ways to make money from AI in 2024

1. **AI Content Generation:** Create AI-powered content generation tools that produce articles, reports, or social media posts.
2. **AI Chatbots:** Develop AI-driven chatbots for customer support or lead generation.
3. **AI SEO Optimization:** Offer AI-based SEO services to enhance website visibility and ranking.
4. **AI Data Labeling:** Provide data labelling services to train AI models, such as image recognition or natural language processing.
5. **AI Data Analysis:** Utilize AI for data analysis and insights to help businesses make informed decisions.
6. **AI Virtual Assistants:** Offer virtual assistants powered by AI for administrative tasks.
7. **AI Personalization:** Develop AI-driven recommendation systems for e-commerce or content platforms.
8. **AI Voice Assistants:** Create voice-activated AI applications for smart devices.
9. **AI Content Curation:** Curate and personalize content for websites and social media using AI algorithms.
10. **AI Video Editing:** Use AI to automate editing, enhancing efficiency and quality.
11. **AI Music Composition:** Develop AI algorithms for composing music for

various purposes, including advertising and entertainment.

12. **AI Stock Trading:** Create AI-powered stock trading algorithms to optimize investments.

13. **AI Image Editing:** Build AI tools for enhancing and retouching images automatically.

14. **AI Language Translation:** Offer AI-based language translation services for websites, documents, and apps.

15. **AI E-Learning:** Develop AI-driven e-learning platforms for personalized educational experiences.

16. **AI Medical Diagnosis:** Build AI models for medical image analysis and diagnostic support.

17. **AI Real Estate Predictions:** Develop AI models to predict real estate market trends and property values.

18. **AI Cybersecurity:** Offer AI-based cybersecurity solutions to protect businesses from threats.

19. **AI Social Media Analytics:** Create AI tools for analyzing social media data to guide marketing strategies.

20. **AI Gaming:** Develop AI-powered games or components, such as intelligent non-player characters (NPCs).

21. **AI Legal Services:** Offer AI-driven legal research and contract analysis services.

22. **AI Copywriting:** Create AI-powered copywriting tools for marketing and advertising content.

23. **AI Sentiment Analysis:** Develop AI sentiment analysis tools for understanding public opinion and market trends.

24. **AI Sports Analytics:** Provide AI-driven sports analytics for teams and individual athletes.

25. **AI Fashion Recommendations:** Develop AI algorithms for personalized fashion recommendations.

26. **AI Healthcare Predictive Analytics:** Offer predictive analytics for healthcare outcomes and disease prevention.

27. **AI Traffic Management:** Create AI systems for optimizing traffic flow and reducing congestion.

28. **AI Energy Management:** Use AI to optimize energy consumption in buildings and industrial processes.

29. **AI Language Tutoring:** Offer AI-based language tutoring services for learners of different languages.

30. **AI Resume Screening:** Provide AI-driven resume screening and candidate matching for recruitment.

31. **AI Insurance Underwriting:** Develop AI models for insurance underwriting and risk assessment.

32. **AI Augmented Reality:** Create AI-powered augmented reality experiences and applications.

33. **AI Chat Fiction:** Write and publish AI-generated chat fiction books or stories.

34. **AI Personal Fitness Coaches:** Develop AI fitness apps that offer personalized workout and nutrition plans.

35. **AI Natural Disaster Prediction:** Use AI for early warning and prediction of natural disasters.

36. **AI Behavioral Analysis:** Provide AI tools for analyzing and predicting human behaviour for various industries.

37. **AI Event Planning:** Utilize AI to assist in event planning and management.

38. **AI Personal Shopping Assistants:** Create AI-driven shopping assistants that help users find the best deals and products.

39. **AI Speech Recognition:** Offer AI speech recognition services for transcription and voice commands.

40. **AI Agriculture Solutions:** Develop AI tools for precision agriculture, crop monitoring, and yield optimization.

41. **AI Psychological Counseling:** Provide AI-driven virtual psychological counselling and therapy.

42. **AI Supply Chain Optimization:** Use AI for supply chain management and optimization.

43. **AI Crowdsourced Data Labeling:** Establish a platform for crowdsourced AI data labelling services.

44. **AI Drone Services:** Offer AI-powered drone services for various applica-

tions, such as aerial photography and surveying.

45. **AI Disaster Recovery:** Develop AI-driven solutions for disaster recovery and business continuity.

46. **AI Food Delivery Optimization:** Use AI to optimize delivery routes and schedules.

47. **AI Digital Marketing Analytics:** Provide AI-driven marketing analytics to optimize digital advertising campaigns.

48. **AI Car Insurance:** Create AI-based car insurance pricing models and risk assessment.

49. **AI Wildlife Conservation:** Utilize AI for wildlife monitoring, anti-poaching efforts, and habitat preservation.

50. **AI Weather Forecasting:** Offer AI-enhanced weather forecasting services for accuracy and precision.

51. **AI Home Energy Efficiency:** Create AI systems for optimizing home energy usage.

52. **AI Social Impact Assessments:** Use AI to assess the social impact of policies, programs, and projects.

53. **AI Equity Research:** Develop AI algorithms for financial equity research and investment recommendations.

54. **AI Geospatial Analysis:** Provide AI geospatial analysis for urban planning and resource management.

55. **AI Mental Health Chatbots:** Create AI-driven chatbots for mental health support and well-being.

56. **AI Robotics Consulting:** Offer consulting services for AI-driven robotics and automation solutions.

57. **AI Eco-Friendly Technologies:** Develop AI solutions for green and sustainable technologies.

58. **AI Non-Profit Fundraising:** Use AI for optimizing fundraising efforts and donor engagement.

59. **AI Life Coaching:** Provide AI-based life coaching services for personal development and goal setting.

60. **AI Archaeological Discovery:** Utilize AI for archaeological site mapping and artefact identification.

61. **AI Crime Prediction:** Develop AI models for predicting and preventing criminal activities.

62. **AI Smart Home Security:** Offer AI-driven smart home security solutions for homeowners.

63. **AI Restaurant Recommendation:** Create AI-powered restaurant recommendation apps based on user preferences.

64. **AI Drone Racing:** Organize and host AI-powered drone racing events and competitions.

65. **AI Space Exploration:** Contribute to AI research and solutions for space exploration missions.

66. **AI Regulatory Compliance:** Offer AI solutions to help businesses comply with regulations and industry standards.

67. **AI Disaster Response:** Develop AI systems for coordinating disaster response efforts and resource allocation.

68. **AI Language Localization:** Provide AI-driven language localization services for apps, websites, and content.

69. **AI Wildlife Photography:** Use AI to develop wildlife photography drones and cameras with tracking capabilities.

70. **AI Trading Bots:** Create AI-powered trading bots for cryptocurrency and stock markets.

71. **AI Language Interpretation:** Offer AI language interpretation services for international business meetings and events.

72. **AI Blockchain Solutions:** Develop AI-enhanced blockchain solutions for various industries, including finance and supply chain.

73. **AI Personal Finance:** Create AI-driven apps to help users manage their finances.

74. **AI Virtual Tours:** Develop AI-driven virtual tour guides for museums, historical sites, and travel destinations.

75. **AI Health Monitoring:** Offer AI-based health monitoring services for early detection of health issues.

76. **AI Sustainable Agriculture:** Develop AI systems for sustainable and eco-friendly agriculture practices.

77. **AI Legal Research:** Provide AI tools for legal research, case analysis, and

contract review.

78. **AI Wildlife Conservation Tourism:** Organize AI-powered wildlife conservation tours and experiences.

79. **AI Video Game Testing:** Use AI for automated testing and quality assurance in video game development.

80. **AI Regulatory Reporting:** Offer AI solutions for automated regulatory reporting in the financial industry.

81. **AI Museums and Exhibits:** Create AI-enhanced interactive exhibits for museums and cultural institutions.

82. **AI Data Security:** Develop AI solutions for data security and business threat detection.

83. **AI Voice Synthesis:** Offer AI voice synthesis services for personalized voiceovers and narration.

84. **AI Real Estate Virtual Tours:** Create AI-driven virtual tours for real estate listings.

85. **AI Crisis Response:** Use AI for crisis management, including natural disasters and emergency services.

86. **AI Children's Education:** Develop AI-driven educational apps and content for children.

87. **AI Sustainable Fashion:** Utilize AI for sustainable fashion design and production.

88. **AI Astronomy and Astrophysics:** Contribute to AI research in astronomy and astrophysics.

89. **AI Renewable Energy:** Create AI solutions for optimizing renewable energy production and consumption.

90. **AI Political Campaigns:** Provide AI tools for data analysis and strategy planning in political campaigns.

91. **AI Smart Appliances:** Develop AI-enhanced smart appliances for homes and kitchens.

92. **AI Drone Surveying:** Offer AI-driven drone surveying services for construction and land management.

93. **AI Remote Work Solutions:** Create AI tools for optimizing remote work and team collaboration.

94. **AI Travel Planning:** Develop AI-driven travel planning apps for personalized itineraries.

95. **AI Cultural Preservation:** Use AI to preserve cultural heritage, languages, and traditions.

96. **AI Emotional Intelligence:** Provide AI-driven emotional intelligence coaching and training.

97. **AI Renewable Energy Forecasting:** Develop AI models for renewable energy production forecasting.

98. **AI Documentary Filmmaking:** Create AI-assisted documentary filmmaking tools and editing.

99. **AI Climate Change Solutions:** Utilize AI for climate modelling, carbon footprint analysis, and climate change mitigation.

100. **AI Space Tourism:** Explore AI applications in the emerging field of space tourism and travel.

101. **AI Disability Assistance:** Develop AI solutions for assisting individuals with disabilities in daily life.

102. **AI Content Moderation:** Offer AI content moderation services to ensure online content compliance.

103. **AI Virtual Events:** Create AI-driven virtual event platforms for conferences, trade shows, and entertainment.

104. **AI Sustainable Transportation:** Develop AI solutions for optimizing public transportation and reducing emissions.

105. **AI Aquaculture:** Utilize AI for sustainable fish and seafood farming.

106. **AI Clean Energy Storage:** Work on AI solutions for efficient energy storage and distribution.

107. **AI Language Learning:** Create AI-driven language learning apps and platforms.

108. **AI Eco-Friendly Architecture:** Use AI for sustainable and eco-friendly architectural design.

109. **AI Livestock Farming:** Develop AI solutions for efficient and humane livestock farming practices.

110. **AI Music Streaming Recommendations:** Offer AI-powered music streaming platforms with personalized recommendations.

111. **AI Cultural Experiences:** Develop AI-enhanced virtual cultural experiences for education and tourism.

112. **AI Travel Safety:** Create AI travel safety apps for real-time alerts and guidance.

113. **AI Resume Review:** Develop AI tools for optimizing and reviewing job resumes for candidates.

114. **AI Health and Fitness Apps:** Create AI-driven health and fitness apps that provide personalized workout and nutrition plans.

115. **AI Virtual Reality Tours:** Offer AI-driven virtual reality tours of historical sites, travel destinations, and real estate properties.

116. **AI Language Translation for Content Creation:** Use AI to translate and adapt content for a global audience.

117. **AI Wildlife Conservation Data Analysis:** Provide AI solutions for analyzing wildlife conservation data and trends.

118. **AI Personalized Fashion Design:** Offer AI-driven personalized fashion design services based on individual style preferences.

119. **AI Elderly Care Solutions:** Develop AI systems to assist in elderly care, such as fall detection and health monitoring.

120. **AI Nonprofit Fundraising:** Utilize AI for data-driven fundraising campaigns and donor engagement.

121. **AI Water Quality Monitoring:** Create AI-powered systems for monitoring and ensuring water quality.

122. **AI Aviation Safety:** Develop AI solutions for enhancing aviation safety and maintenance.

123. **AI Sports Performance Analysis:** Offer AI-driven sports performance analysis for athletes and teams.

124. **AI Environmental Impact Assessment:** Use AI for assessing the environmental impact of projects and initiatives.

125. **AI Pet Care and Training:** Develop AI solutions for pet care, training, and behaviour analysis.

126. **AI Parenting Assistance:** Create AI apps and services to assist parents in child-rearing and development.

127. **AI Photography Enhancements:** Offer AI-based tools for enhancing and

retouching photos.

128. **AI Freelance Platforms:** Develop AI-powered freelance platforms that match freelancers with suitable projects.

129. **AI Mental Health Support:** Create AI-driven mental health and emotional well-being support services.

130. **AI Health Diagnostics:** Develop AI systems for early health diagnostics and self-assessment.

131. **AI Investment Analysis:** Provide AI-driven investment analysis and portfolio optimization tools.

132. **AI Car Maintenance:** Offer AI-based car maintenance and diagnostics services for vehicle owners.

133. **AI Food Delivery Optimization:** Develop AI systems for optimizing food delivery routes and times.

134. **AI Event Planning:** Use AI for event planning, venue selection, and vendor recommendations.

135. **AI Microbrewery Brewing:** Create AI-enhanced brewing systems for microbreweries.

136. **AI Remote Sensing:** Develop AI solutions for remote sensing and data collection in agriculture and forestry.

137. **AI Solar Energy Optimization:** Offer AI-based solutions for optimizing solar energy systems.

138. **AI Sustainability Auditing:** Provide AI sustainability auditing services for businesses and organizations.

139. **AI Personalized News Aggregators:** Create AI news aggregators that deliver personalized news content to users.

140. **AI Genealogy Research:** Use AI for genealogy research and ancestral history tracing.

141. **AI Personalized Learning Platforms:** Develop AI-driven personalized learning platforms for students and professionals.

142. **AI Natural Disaster Prediction:** Create AI models for predicting natural disasters and extreme weather events.

143. **AI Drone Delivery Services:** Offer AI-powered drone delivery services for businesses and consumers.

144. **AI Aquatic Life Monitoring:** Develop AI systems for monitoring aquatic ecosystems and marine life.

145. **AI Voice-Controlled Smart Home Systems:** Create AI-based voice-controlled smart home systems for convenience and security.

146. **AI Sustainable Transportation Planning:** Utilize AI for planning sustainable transportation options in urban areas.

147. **AI Wildlife Rehabilitation:** Develop AI systems for wildlife rehabilitation and tracking.

148. **AI Climate Change Adaptation:** Provide AI solutions for adaptation and mitigation strategies.

149. **AI Fitness Coaching Chatbots:** Offer AI chatbots that provide fitness coaching and motivation.

150. **AI Sustainable Food Production:** Use AI for optimizing sustainable food production practices.

151. **AI E-Learning for Special Needs:** Create AI-driven e-learning platforms for individuals with special needs.

152. **AI Indigenous Language Preservation:** Utilize AI for preserving and revitalizing indigenous languages.

153. **AI Pollution Monitoring:** Develop AI systems for monitoring air and water pollution levels.

154. **AI Real-time Language Translation Devices:** Create AI devices for real-time language translation and communication.

155. **AI Disaster Recovery Solutions:** Offer AI-driven disaster recovery and data backup solutions for businesses.

156. **AI Virtual Assistant for the Elderly:** Develop AI virtual assistants tailored to the needs of elderly individuals.

157. **AI Sustainable Agriculture Consulting:** Provide AI consulting services for sustainable agriculture practices.

158. **AI Public Safety Apps:** Create AI-driven public safety apps for reporting and addressing safety concerns.

159. **AI Renewable Energy Consultation:** Offer AI-based consultations for implementing renewable energy solutions.

160. **AI Sustainable Tourism:** Utilize AI to promote sustainable and responsi-

ble tourism practices.

161. **AI Mobile Health Apps:** Develop AI mobile apps for health monitoring and telemedicine.

162. **AI Traffic Management:** Create AI systems for optimizing traffic flow and reducing congestion.

163. **AI Event Ticket Pricing Optimization:** Use AI to optimize event ticket pricing for organizers.

164. **AI Virtual Classroom for Lifelong Learning:** Develop AI virtual classrooms for continuous and lifelong learning.

165. **AI Eco-Friendly Packaging:** Create AI solutions for eco-friendly packaging and materials.

166. **AI Sustainable Urban Planning:** Develop AI systems for optimizing urban planning to enhance sustainability and quality of life.

167. **AI Wildlife Conservation Drones:** Use AI in drones for monitoring and protecting wildlife and ecosystems.

168. **AI Language Tutoring:** Create AI-driven language tutoring apps for learners of all ages.

169. **AI Marine Exploration:** Utilize AI in underwater robots and submarines for marine exploration and research.

170. **AI Pest Control:** Develop AI solutions for pest control in agriculture, reducing the need for pesticides.

171. **AI Personalized Travel Planning:** Offer AI-powered travel planning services tailored to individual preferences and interests.

172. **AI Accessibility Tools:** Create AI tools for improving accessibility for disabled individuals.

173. **AI Virtual Reality Therapy:** Use AI-driven virtual reality for therapeutic interventions and mental health support.

174. **AI Property Management:** Provide AI-based property management services for real estate owners.

175. **AI Sustainable Fashion Brands:** Start sustainable fashion brands with AI-optimized designs and supply chain processes.

176. **AI Geospatial Analytics:** Develop AI systems for geospatial data analysis and mapping.

177. **AI Personalized Art Creation:** Offer AI-generated personalized artwork and design services.

178. **AI Aquaculture Management:** Use AI to optimize aquaculture operations and seafood production.

179. **AI Personalized Marketing Content:** Create AI-driven marketing content tailored to individual customer preferences.

180. **AI Biodiversity Monitoring:** Develop AI tools for monitoring and preserving ecosystem biodiversity.

181. **AI Sustainable Building Design:** Utilize AI for designing energy-efficient and sustainable buildings.

182. **AI Customized Wellness Plans:** Provide AI-driven wellness plans and recommendations based on individual health data.

183. **AI Adaptive Gaming:** Create AI-enhanced video games that adapt to players' skills and preferences.

184. **AI Personalized Podcasts:** Offer AI-generated personalized podcast content and recommendations.

185. **AI Crop Disease Detection:** Develop AI systems for early detection of crop diseases in agriculture.

186. **AI Green Energy Consulting:** Provide AI-based consultations for adopting green and renewable energy solutions.

187. **AI Personalized Financial Planning:** Use AI to offer personalized financial planning and investment strategies.

188. **AI Ecosystem Restoration:** Utilize AI in ecosystem restoration and reforestation initiatives.

189. **AI Sustainable Transportation Services:** Create AI-powered services for sustainable transportation options.

190. **AI Personalized Mental Health Apps:** Develop AI-driven mental health apps tailored to individual needs.

191. **AI Wildlife Rehabilitation and Release:** Use AI in wildlife rehabilitation programs to monitor animals' progress.

192. **AI Sustainable Waste Management:** Provide AI solutions for optimizing waste reduction and recycling processes.

193. **AI Personalized Art Curation:** Offer AI-curated art collections based on

individual tastes and preferences.

194. **AI Freshwater Conservation:** Develop AI systems for preserving and managing freshwater resources.

195. **AI Sustainable Product Design:** Create eco-friendly products and designs with AI-driven optimization.

196. **AI Personalized Book Recommendations:** Use AI to offer personalized book recommendations and reading lists.

197. **AI Food Waste Reduction:** Develop AI systems for reducing food waste in supply chains and kitchens.

198. **AI Personalized Mental Health Chatbots:** Create AI chatbots for mental health support and conversations.

199. **AI Green Certification Services:** Provide AI-based certifications for environmentally friendly products and practices.

200. **AI Sustainable Tourism Experiences:** Offer AI-enhanced sustainable travel experiences and tours.

201. **AI Personalized Fitness Equipment:** Create AI-powered fitness equipment and workout programs.

202. **AI Climate Data Analysis:** Develop AI systems for analyzing climate data and trends.

203. **AI Sustainable Packaging Design:** Use AI for designing eco-friendly packaging and materials.

204. **AI Virtual Art Galleries:** Create AI-driven virtual galleries for showcasing and selling artwork.

205. **AI Marine Pollution Detection:** Develop AI tools for monitoring and mitigating marine pollution.

206. **AI Sustainable Farming Practices:** Provide AI consulting for sustainable farming and agriculture.

207. **AI Virtual Life Coaches:** Create AI-driven virtual life coaching and self-improvement programs.

208. **AI Sustainable Forestry Management:** Use AI for optimizing sustainable forestry practices.

209. **AI Personalized Home Decor:** Offer AI-generated home decor and interior design recommendations.

210. **AI Mental Health and Wellness Blogs:** Create AI-driven blogs and content on mental health and wellness.

211. **AI Sustainable Water Management:** Develop AI systems for efficient water resource management and conservation.

212. **AI Personalized Travel Apps:** Create AI-powered travel apps that customize itineraries and recommendations for travellers.

213. **AI Biometric Security:** Provide AI-based biometric security solutions for businesses and individuals.

214. **AI Sustainable Agriculture Consulting:** Offer AI consulting services for sustainable and eco-friendly agriculture practices.

215. **AI Emotional Intelligence Training:** Develop AI-driven programs to enhance emotional intelligence in individuals and teams.

216. **AI Remote Sensing:** Use AI for remote sensing applications in agriculture, forestry, and climate monitoring.

217. **AI Personalized Content Creation Tools:** Create AI tools for personalized content generation, including articles, videos, and music.

218. **AI Sustainable Energy Storage:** Develop AI solutions for optimizing energy storage systems in renewable energy.

219. **AI Self-Driving Delivery Services:** Offer AI-powered autonomous delivery services for goods and packages.

220. **AI Sustainable Packaging Consulting:** Provide AI-driven recommendations for sustainable packaging solutions.

221. **AI Personalized Home Renovation:** Use AI to offer personalized home renovation and improvement plans.

222. **AI Crisis Management and Disaster Response:** Develop AI systems for efficient disaster response and management.

223. **AI Sustainable Fishing Practices:** Offer AI consulting for sustainable and responsible fishing practices.

224. **AI Personalized Clothing Design:** Create AI-driven clothing design services based on individual styles and preferences.

225. **AI Personalized Nutrition Plans:** Develop AI-generated nutrition plans tailored to individual health goals.

226. **AI Sustainability Certification:** Provide AI-based certifications for eco-

friendly and sustainable businesses.

227. **AI Personalized Travel Apparel:** Offer AI-curated travel clothing and gear recommendations.

228. **AI Sustainable Water Purification:** Use AI to optimize water purification and treatment processes.

229. **AI Personalized E-Learning:** Create AI-driven e-learning platforms that adapt to individual learning styles.

230. **AI Wildlife Data Analysis:** Develop AI systems for analyzing wildlife data and conservation efforts.

231. **AI Sustainable Tourism Marketing:** Offer AI-powered marketing services for sustainable tourism businesses.

232. **AI Personalized Culinary Experiences:** Provide AI-curated culinary experiences and recipes.

233. **AI Sustainable Supply Chain Management:** Use AI to optimize eco-friendly supply chain and logistics.

234. **AI Personalized Career Coaching:** Develop AI-driven career coaching programs based on individual aspirations.

235. **AI Sustainable Mining Practices:** Offer AI consulting for sustainable and responsible mining operations.

236. **AI Personalized Gaming Experiences:** Create AI-enhanced personalized gaming experiences and content.

237. **AI Sustainable Transportation Consulting:** Provide AI-based advice for sustainable transportation solutions.

238. **AI Personalized Gift Recommendations:** Offer AI-curated gift recommendations for special occasions.

239. **AI Sustainable Urban Design:** Use AI for designing sustainable and eco-friendly urban environments.

240. **AI Personalized Pet Care:** Develop AI tools for personalized pet care and recommendations.

241. **AI Sustainable Tourism Apps:** Create AI-powered apps for sustainable travel and tourism.

242. **AI Personalized Home Fitness Programs:** Offer AI-generated fitness programs tailored to individual goals.

243. **AI Sustainable Architecture:** Utilize AI in sustainable architectural design and construction.

244. **AI Personalized Digital Art:** Create AI-generated personalized digital art pieces.

245. **AI Sustainable Shipping Solutions:** Provide AI-driven solutions for eco-friendly shipping and cargo transportation.

246. **AI Personalized Event Planning:** Use AI for personalized event planning services and recommendations.

247. **AI Sustainable Waste Recycling:** Develop AI systems for optimizing waste recycling processes.

248. **AI Personalized Mental Health Journals:** Offer AI-driven mental health journaling and self-improvement platforms.

249. **AI Sustainable Tourism Reviews:** Create AI-powered platforms for eco-friendly travel and accommodation reviews.

250. **AI Personalized Fashion Accessories:** Develop AI-curated fashion accessory recommendations.

251. **AI Sustainable Fisheries Management:** Use AI for optimizing sustainable fisheries and fish population management.

252. **AI Personalized Travel Photography:** Offer AI-curated travel photography recommendations.

253. **AI Sustainable Textile Production:** Provide AI solutions for eco-friendly textile manufacturing processes.

254. **AI Personalized Learning Toys:** Create AI-enhanced personalized educational toys for children.

255. **AI Personalized Skin Care:** Develop AI-generated personalized skincare routines and product recommendations.

Conclusion

As we close the book on "AI Secrets for the Creator Economy: 200+ Proven Ways to Make Money from AI in 2024 and Beyond," it's important to reflect on the dramatic transition we've undergone. This book has guided you through the perilous terrain of the Creator Economy, where human inventiveness and artificial intelligence meet to redefine success and prosperity.

The Creator Economy, an ever-expanding digital cosmos, has reached new heights, and AI is unmistakably at the helm. Creators of various types have found their niches in this ecosystem, transforming their interests into viable companies. Entrepreneurship has transformed, with innovators now holding the reins of wealth generation.

2024 marks a watershed moment in this ecosystem, with AI cementing its crucial role. AI is more than a tool; it is a catalyst for creativity, a multiplier of efficiency, and a monetization accelerator. It is an active collaborator, working alongside creators to make their visions a reality.

Through the pages of this book, we've unlocked the rich trove of "AI Secrets for the Creator Economy." This resource has provided you with more than just information; it has also served as your entry point into the AI environment. From fundamental principles to complex applications, it keeps you at the cutting edge of AI expertise in an ever-changing landscape.

We've looked into various possibilities, revealing how AI might boost wealth creation in the Creator Economy. We've discussed content production, audience engagement, monetization techniques, entrepreneurship, and how to prepare for a career in the Creator Economy. It's been a voyage of creativity, invention, and financial success.

AI secrets offer success and fulfilment in the Creator Economy of 2024 and beyond. You embark on a transforming journey when you finish the final chapter of this book. The AI secrets you've discovered will unlock a future where innovation, creativity, and financial success will intersect to exceed your most ambitious goals.

It's important to remember that it's not just about business but also responsible AI usage and ethical navigation. As we progress, we must address the ethical implications of our actions to ensure that the incredible power of AI is used for the greater good.

You hold the keys to unlocking a future limited only by your creativity in this age of innovation, where AI and the Creator Economy have become inseparable friends. The AI secrets are yours to wield, to shape your route to success, to build your vision, and to forge your destiny in a world where the Creator Economy knows no limitations.

As you take your first steps, remember that the future is yours to mould, and the AI secrets you carry with you are the guiding stars on your journey to riches and fulfilment. It's time to embrace the limitless possibilities that await in the Creator Economy, fuelled by AI's immense potential.

Also by Glorioustina Essia

Unveiling Cybersecurity Governance: Building a Strong Foundation: A Comprehensive Guide to Cybersecurity Governance and Compliance (Book 1)

In the ever-expanding digital landscape, safeguarding sensitive information and maintaining robust cyberse-curity practices have become paramount. "Unveiling Cybersecurity Governance: Building a Strong Foundation" is a comprehensive guide that delves into the core principles and components of cybersecurity governance, equipping readers with the knowledge and tools to establish a secure digital environment.

THE GUARDIANS OF SECURITY: EXPLORING THE ROLE OF GOVERNANCE: Strengthening Cybersecurity Gover-nance A Comprehensive Guide to Cybersecurity Gover-nance and Compliance (Book 2)

Step into a world where cybersecurity governance serves as a catalyst for a secure future. Explore the realms of "The Guardians of Security: Exploring the Role of Governance," the much awaited second book in the epic series "Secure Horizons: A Comprehensive Guide to Cybersecurity Governance and Compliance."

As you read each page of "The Guardians of Security," prepare to be enchanted by the author's remarkable storytelling ability. This book presents a vivid picture of the complicated landscape of cybersecurity governance with a seamless blend of real-world experiences, cutting-edge research, and visionary concepts. Immerse yourself in an exciting story that uncovers the brains and souls of people dedicated to defending our digital borders.

www.ingramcontent.com/pod-product-compliance
Lightning Source LLC
LaVergne TN
LVHW051658050326
832903LV00032B/3877